Praise for *Future Millionaire*

"Rachel Rodgers blends financial savvy with heart and humor. *Future Millionaire* is the perfect companion for young people who want to live better, dream bigger, and take charge of their lives."

—Tiffany Aliche, *New York Times* bestselling author of *Get Good with Money*

"Rachel Rodgers's *Future Millionaire* is a must-read for the next gen as they aim to make sense of their money and create a genuine path to wealth."

—Farnoosh Torabi, host of *So Money* and author of *A Healthy State of Panic*

"Rachel Rodgers is living proof that your mindset and financial habits can help you thrive. One of my only regrets is not having this knowledge earlier, but the next generation has the opportunity to benefit from her step-by-step guide!"

—Angela Yee, American radio personality

"Rachel Rodgers turns young readers into leaders. *Future Millionaire* shows you how to step up, make smart decisions, and create a life of abundance."

—Minda Harts, speaker, bestselling author, and founder and CEO of The Memo

"*Future Millionaire* is a game-changer for young people who dream big and want to make those dreams happen. This book isn't just about wealth—it's about empowerment, mindset, and taking actionable steps to secure a prosperous future. It's perfect for anyone ready to break barriers, defy the odds, and create a life they're proud of. I wish I had this guide when I was starting out—this is the blueprint for building generational wealth and success."

—Hala Taha, host of the *Young and Profiting Podcast*, CEO and founder of YAP Media and YAP Media Podcast Network

Future MILLIONAIRE

A Young Person's Step-by-Step Guide to Making WEALTH Inevitable

RACHEL RODGERS

BLINK

"I've learned that making a 'living' is not the same thing as making a 'life.'"

—MAYA ANGELOU

This book is dedicated to all my children . . . Adzua, Alexa, Chance, Fatia, Jackson, Jasmine, Jettstorm, Kalash, Maxwell, Mercy, Riley, Tyler, and every child and young person in the world who will one day try to make it. Here's a spoiler alert: you will make it. My hope is that this book shows you not only how to make a living, but how to make a joyful, adventurous, love-filled life at the same time.

XO,

R

BLINK

Future Millionaire

Published in Grand Rapids, Michigan, by Blink.

Requests for information should be addressed to customercare@harpercollins.com.

ISBN 978-0-310-15820-2 (hardcover)
ISBN 978-0-310-17916-0 (ITPE)
ISBN 978-0-310-15813-4 (audio)
ISBN 978-0-310-15811-0 (ebook)

Library of Congress Cataloging-in-Publication Data is available.

Cover Design: Patti Evans
Cover Photography: Dale May
Interior Design: Denise Froehlich

Printed in the United States of America

25 26 27 28 29 LBC 5 4 3 2 1

Contents

INTRODUCTION

You don't have any money.

I didn't either.

Not only did I not *have* any money, I had no clue how to *get* any money.

Nevertheless, I am a millionaire. And you? You are a Future Millionaire.

By the time you finish reading this book, you will know and believe that this is true about yourself. Not only will you fully accept your identity as a Future Millionaire, you will have a plan and the mindset to make it happen.

You see, getting money is a learnable skill. And I am about to teach it to you.

First lesson: You're not broke, you're pre-rich.

You are a Future Millionaire. Declare it. Know it. Demand it. Of yourself and the world.

And prepare to work for it.

No, it's not the kind of work you're thinking. It's not *"all my life, grindin' all my life"*–type work. It's *taking a risk/putting yourself out there/asking for the sale*–type work. But don't worry about all that right now. We'll get into it later.

All you need to know right now is that no matter what your life or bank account looks like today, you *can* be wealthy. I'll even go so far to say: baby, you *will* be wealthy. As long as you trust and believe that it's possible, I believe it for you. But you have to believe it for yourself.

And I'm not talking about just saying it out loud and then hoping millions magically appear in your bank account one day. Canvas bags with dollar signs are not gonna suddenly fall from the sky and bust you in the head, no matter how many times you've seen that in cartoons. There will be work. Effort is required. The right mindset is required. But wealth is possible. And if you truly believe, wealth is probable.

Being young might feel like a setback on your journey toward wealth. Maybe you feel like your ideas and skills aren't taken seriously yet. Maybe you feel like you lack access to the people who could really help you. Maybe you feel like making money—*real* money, not part-time, sweatin'-it-out-for-minimum-wage money—simply isn't possible when you're young. Or when you're young and a person of color. Or when you're young and identify as LGBTQIA+. Or when you're young and you grew up low income, or middle class, or you live in an expensive city, or a small town, or out in the country. You might feel the way you look or the way you talk is preventing you from being wealthy.

You are right that some people won't take you seriously. You are right that some people are racist. Some people are sexist. Some people are homophobic. Some people are transphobic. Some people are fatphobic. And some people are jerks.

Some of these issues are institutional and systemic. For example, as a young Black woman, I had a hard time getting a business loan for my first company. Studies show that banking policies are sexist and racist. Depending on your identity, these are very real barriers you may contend with on your journey to build wealth. But that's no secret, right? You're living that truth already. Despite those very real barriers, I still became a wealthy Black woman. And you can become a wealthy young person, a wealthy woman, a wealthy queer person, a wealthy person of color, a wealthy disabled person.

The real secret is that having wealth isn't just about the money. It's about what you can do with that money. What would you do with an extra $5,000? $10,000? $100,000? Or $1,000,000?

Would you pay off your parents' mortgage so they never have to stress about paying that bill ever again? Would you buy your sister a car so she can stop taking the bus late at night? Would you stop taking out student loans and pay for the rest of college with the cash you have? Would you provide toys at Christmas and back-to-school supplies in the fall for low-income kids in your neighborhood? Would you back progressive political candidates that you believe in? Would you send a food truck to feed protesters fighting for a cause you care about?

> Ask yourself: What would be possible if I was earning a lot more money?

Money is not about the money. It's about how that money can be used to make your life better, make your loved ones' lives better, and make the people in your community's lives better. It's about gaining social, economic, and political power that enables your voice to be heard and your dollars to be used to create the world you actually want to live in.

It's also about belief—specifically, the things you believe about yourself. It's about the barriers that hold people back, and it's about your daily habits, all of which we'll get into in this book. But the *most* important thing about building wealth is that **you have to believe in yourself.**

That is the best investment you can ever make.

You may be thinking, *Why should I listen to you?* Well, for starters, I'm a millionaire. And I made every cent through a business I built with my own two hands. Everything I'm going to tell you to do, I did myself. But I also made a lot of mistakes. I didn't grow up with money. Not even close. I know what it's like to see your parents struggle, to see bills not getting paid, to see the fear and stress on their faces when the landlord is knocking and the rent is late again.

My dad passed away suddenly when I was in seventh grade. For my mom, my older sister, and me, his death threw our lives into chaos. My mom had been with him since she was sixteen; she was lost without him. She basically checked out, swallowed up by her grief. My older sister and my best friend's family looked out for me, but it was scary and sad. I experienced food insecurity up close. (Does it get any closer than not having enough to eat?) I witnessed the power company turning off our lights. I didn't feel safe, because how can you feel safe if it always feels like you might lose your home? I didn't want that for my family, and I didn't want that for my future.

Those experiences taught me that I needed to take control of my life. I needed to make my own money. I needed to seize my own power.

The truth is that money equals security. It equals power. It means being in control of your life. Being able to help yourself and the people you love.

Having money means being able to *make* choices rather than have choices forced on you. Being able to buy groceries *and* get that dope new pair of kicks. Being able to go to a movie with your friends *and* get the mega-size tub of popcorn. (Hell, throw in some Goobers and gigantic sodas too!) Being able to go to college, if you want, and not leave with six figures of debt (like I did). Being able to shoot for the career that makes you happy, not the one that wears you out and still barely pays enough to cover the bills.

I wanted that.

My way out was to become a lawyer. I used to watch courtroom dramas on TV with my mom, and I liked how the lawyers advocated for people. That resonated with me. And I understood that a lawyer was a well-paid and well-respected position. I decided that would be my path to money and security. And while I wasn't wrong, it didn't happen quite like I envisioned. I studied law, worked for a law firm for only a few months, and then boldly chose to open my own law firm. My practice was successful—but on the side, I started coaching other young professionals about how they could also build successful businesses, and I realized that I liked that a lot better. So don't get too caught up in feeling like you have to know what you want to do with your life right from the start of your career. You probably won't.

Law doesn't have to be your path. Entrepreneurialism doesn't have to be your path. If you follow your interests, you'll discover *your* path, but first you have to believe that you deserve to. And you do. You deserve security. You deserve power. You deserve a career you love that pays.

You. Deserve. Wealth.

If you take away nothing else from this book, believe that. No matter where you are now, no matter what your starting point is, you deserve to be financially secure. You deserve to be free.

This book will show you how. First, we'll talk about how to Get Ready.

Before you can bulk up your bank account, you've got to prepare for success. We all have habits and ways of thinking that can get in the way of our goals. We're going to break down what those are, and how to beat them.

In part two, we'll dive into how to Get Money. This is all about the actions you'll take to set yourself up for wealth. We'll talk about how to determine the best career path for you. How to manage your money. How to protect it, and how to invest it.

I'll be honest with you: you'll have to work hard, especially if your upbringing and identity have you at a disadvantage. (No, it's not fair, but it is a fact.) But building wealth is possible for you. And it's definitely worth it. Now let's go get it!

PART ONE:

Get Ready

CHAPTER 1

Dream Like a Millionaire

Money equals mindset. You can't just think your way into being rich—you're going to have to back those thoughts up with action. But you can definitely think yourself into staying poor (by not taking action at all). A healthy money mindset is crucial to building wealth.

Think about it: Having money gives you confidence. You feel more in control. You trust yourself and the choices you're making. You can steer your own ship. That sounds good, right?!

It sure felt good to me as a kid. There was a time when my parents made a comfortable living. My parents bought a two-bedroom condo in a nice building where they finally had their own bedroom. But then, tired of consistently being passed over for promotions after years of hard work, my mother quit her job. A few months later, as (bad) luck would have it, my father was laid off. Next thing we knew, it was food stamps and late rent. My mother had a hard time finding another job of the same caliber, and though she and my father worked hard at the various jobs they did get, our family never regained our financial footing.

Then my father got very sick. He was in and out of the hospital for years. He could not work consistently because of his illness, and I can't imagine what the hospital bills must have been like. Then, at only forty-three years old, he passed away. My mother, older sister, and I were devastated. After my dad died, my mom was in a daze of grief, so my sister got a job and took over the household responsibilities. She would come home tired and stressed, yelling at me for not helping around the house enough. It was a really difficult time for all three of us. And the financial stress only made things feel worse. I'm sure my mom and my sister were scared, and I *know* I was.

Not having money creates fear—fear of never having enough, fear of not being able to pay for the things you want and need, and fear of being judged for it. I distinctly remember that feeling. As a kid, I'd stand in the grocery store checkout line, embarrassed to pay with food stamps. I was terrified that my friends from school might see, that they would realize my family was receiving public assistance.

I understand now that poverty and debt are not things to be ashamed of. They are rarely in most people's control, especially for young people. You're just getting started, and so much about what your life looks like right now has been in the hands of somebody else—your parents, your community, your government, the rules and prejudices that hold people back. Our culture has a messed-up way of looking at poverty. Instead of offering compassion, it's assumed that people with low income are lazy and uneducated. They're seen as unproductive members of society or, worse, social sponges who are all too happy to get by on government handouts. (This was not true for my family or most people I knew who were barely getting by.) The truth is, my parents were very smart and productive. They worked hard, and for a time we lived comfortably. But when our circumstances changed, we got hit hard.

Fear and shame require a lot of energy—energy that you might otherwise direct toward school, sports, a job, college, a career that you love. Fear and shame tell you that you can't: You can't be the kind of person who is able to pay her bills. You can't be the kind of person who lives in a nice home. You can't take trips or eat at fancy restaurants. Fear and shame tell you those things are off-limits to you. Those things are reserved for someone else. And inevitably, your brain fills in the rest: *Those things are for someone better than me.*

When we feel judged by other people, we start seeing ourselves as we imagine they see us. We may even start believing the version of us we think they see. *Maybe being poor* does *mean I'm not worthy. Maybe needing public assistance* does *mean I shouldn't have nice things. Maybe I'm not smart enough to change my situation. Maybe I'm just not the kind of person who'll ever experience financial security. Maybe I'll just always be poor.*

That's 100 percent not true. Your circumstances today do not determine your circumstances tomorrow. There may be forces that have made it harder for you to earn the kind of money you dream of (we'll get into some of those later), but that's not your fault. It's not your family's fault. And it does not define your future.

If you've had any of these thoughts, hear me right now: You. Are. Worthy. You're worthy of wealth, you're worthy of safety, you're worthy of having nice things just because they're nice.

Growing up, a lot of people will try to tell you that you're not.

They're wrong.

This is what you need to absorb, right now. Repeat it to yourself if you want to. Repeat it every day. (I know it feels corny and uncool but do it anyway.) *I deserve success.*

TRY IT: Say this to yourself: **I deserve success.** Say it out loud. **I deserve success.** Own this truth about yourself and don't let anyone convince you otherwise. **I deserve success.** Keep saying it until you believe it. **I deserve success.** Say it, mean it, live it.

Here's the point of letting yourself be a little corny: your present thoughts define your future. What you believe is possible. To start this journey, you first have to open yourself up to the very idea of wealth being possible for you. If you don't believe that, it's going to be real freaking hard to actually achieve it. You'll talk yourself out of doing the work that will be required. You'll tell yourself you wouldn't have gotten that high-paying job even if you had applied. You'll convince yourself that there's no point in putting yourself out there. You'll find endlessly creative ways to sabotage your own chance at success.

But if you believe you can be a millionaire, you *can* be a millionaire. Why? Because when you believe, you'll do the work and put the steps into place that will make that belief a reality. You'll let nothing stop you. And the haters better get out of your way.

After my dad died and everything fell apart, I made foolish choices. I was sad and scared, and I started dating a "bad boy." (News flash: bad boys are bad for you.) I lashed out and drank in the park at night with my friends. I was angry at God for not saving my father, and at my mother for checking out instead of taking care of us.

I might've been on a crash course to disaster, except that I had determined by then that my future would look a lot different than my present. I limited my "acting out" to the weekends. I went to school, studied hard, and kept up my grades. I convinced my school to give me a scholarship for SAT prep classes and stayed focused on my dream of college and then law school. I didn't yet know what a millionaire was, exactly, but I knew I didn't want to have the same financial struggles that were pummeling my family. I got into college, studied hard while also holding down a thirty-hour-per-week job, and eventually landed the chance to intern in the US Senate.

That's one of the many reasons it's so important to make your dream real. Because it's something you can focus on during those times when you otherwise might feel lost and aimless. Your dream keeps you steering in the direction you want to go.

I'll be real with you; it wasn't easy for me. It may not be easy for you either. But I've done it and so can you.

Are you with me? Then it's time to start thinking like a millionaire!

If you haven't grown up with much money, you've probably experienced how it feels to be judged and shamed because of who you are (or rather, who other people think you are) and what you have (or don't have—yet). This is especially true for women and people of color, but it also happens simply because you're young. Based on the assumptions people make about you in the present, they assume that's also your future. That if you're young and broke, you'll never be anything else (except maybe *old* and broke). This sends a message of shame: that we should be embarrassed if we are in debt, if we don't make much money, if we can't pay our bills, if we can't buy what we want and need.

What they *don't* tell you (in fact, what many are working really hard these days to keep you from learning) is that in our society, this is a feature not a bug. If you don't have much money right now, if it feels like opportunities aren't available for somebody "like you," if you feel ashamed because you're broke . . . more likely than not, it's not your fault. And the reasons for your situation have been baked into our systems—and even the laws themselves—to keep you this way.

Let me explain. Only somewhat recently in American life have laws been created to protect marginalized groups' rights to earn and manage their income. We're talking the mid- to late-twentieth century. Before then, laws restricted things like who could own property, who was considered to *be* property, who could have bank accounts, who could take out loans, who could vote, and who could hold public office (and thus, have a say in changing these laws), just to name a few. And you might guess who was primarily making these laws, and who was exempt from these restrictions: white, straight men.

This means that for decades—centuries, even—if you were female, Black, Asian, Native American, Latinx, or some other non-white identity, it's been significantly harder to earn money, buy property with a mortgage, have bank accounts and credit cards, start a business requiring a loan, or make other large purchases such as a car, at least not without a man to cosign with you. Never mind that these folks were usually paid less for their work as well. (Although the Equal Pay Act was passed in 1963, even today women and marginalized groups make significantly less than white men do for the same work.)

Taken together, this means that white men have had a four-hundred-year head start when it comes to creating wealth. This includes wealth accumulated through the labor and suffering of others, most of all Black Americans who were enslaved for 246 years. And it is wealth that they have been able to pass down to their children and grandchildren for generations. This is called a wealth gap, and I probably don't have to tell you that it still persists today. In fact, we should call it a wealth chasm, because it was created over centuries and will likely take centuries to close.

Women and folks in systemically marginalized communities have been held back in other ways too. Being a parent is wonderful, but historically, raising children has created far more disadvantages for women than men. So too for people who aren't thin, or who are LGBTQIA+. (Research backs this up.) Discrimination is more than emotionally hurtful; it's economically harmful as well. Think about how discrimination affects a person's ability to get into college, as well as their job opportunities, starting salary and/or chance at a promotion, and access to capital to start a business, just to name a few. This is all to say, these systems have been in place for way longer than you or I have been around.

The next time you find yourself thinking, *I'm not good with money* or *People like me don't make a lot of money,* think about some of the reasons why that might be.

> **The next time you find yourself thinking, *I'm not good with money* or *People like me don't make a lot of money,* think about some of the reasons why that might be.**

Literally centuries' worth of laws, customs, and widespread behavior have created the conditions for you to have less. They're so deeply ingrained in our culture that they may affect your life and bank account in ways you might not even realize. Certainly, it has made many of us believe that becoming wealthy is out of reach for us.

Yes, that's a lot. But it doesn't mean things are hopeless. As we've already discussed, **you are not stuck**. Let's end the cycle now, you and me. Let's stop beating ourselves up for what's been beyond our control, what's been beyond our ancestors' control. Let's stop letting others tell us that doing the best we can—taking out student loans, accepting government aid, using credit cards, not knowing how to negotiate a larger salary—is our fault. Be gentle with yourself. Hell, give yourself a big ol' pat on the back for picking up this book in the first place. Even if the deck has been stacked against you, you're here reading this book, ready to up your financial game. Your decision to learn, to find a way, is a Million Dollar Decision. Let's make it count.

You might have picked up this book because you really want to learn how to manage your money. And you will! But first I want you to learn how to *think* about money. And that starts with opening your mind and letting yourself dream big. We need big dreams so we don't limit ourselves to only what we currently think is possible for us. Most people are capable of so much more than they allow themselves to believe.

Million Dollar Decision: *(noun)* A decision that moves you toward abundance and away from scarcity. Specifically, a MDD is one that: frees up your time and energy so you can devote them to the things that move you toward your goals; reduces the demands on your mental space; builds you up and makes you feel strong, independent, and able to make the choices you *want* to make in your life; and opens up opportunities.

When I started my first business, a law firm, all I wanted to do was replace my $41,000-per-year salary and be able to afford health insurance. That was the extent of my dreams. But guess what? I accomplished that in less than twelve months! When I started, I didn't realize how safe my so-called dream was. I didn't realize that I was afraid to set big goals, and I set a goal that was really achievable. In other words, I was phoning it in. When I quickly achieved it, I needed a bigger dream.

I then set my sights on making $100,000. Six figures sounded like a lot. But in the next year, I far exceeded that goal. I made over $300,000 in my second year of business! Then I felt a bit lost and confused for a while because I didn't have a clear goal. I continued to make about the same amount of money for almost three years. Eventually, I got up the courage to say: I want a million! It took me seven years to achieve my first million-dollar year. It probably would have happened a lot faster if I'd had the audacity to dream of a million sooner.

Allowing yourself to dream is a prerequisite to getting rich. You're expanding the limits your brain currently has set. What do you believe is possible for yourself? What's beyond your wildest dreams? A lot of people are afraid to say what they want because they think it's not possible, or they fear that people will judge them for having a lofty goal. They're afraid to dream big and then fall short.

Don't be that person.

There's no harm in dreaming a Million Dollar Dream. Even if you end up achieving a $500k dream, you still pushed yourself beyond where you were before. So go for it; don't hold back! Dream your biggest dream. Right now. Nobody's watching. If you don't know what that dream is yet, give it some thought. If you were to have all the resources you need—maybe it's money, maybe it's connections, or time, or a particular skill, or living in the right location, or reaching the right audience—what would you want to do?

Million Dollar Dream: *(noun)* Your highest and best vision for your life, outlining exactly what you want for yourself, down to the smallest detail. A Million Dollar Dream gives you the full picture of how you want to work, live, and play, who you want to spend your time with, how much money you want to make, and what experiences you want to have. When imagining your Million Dollar Dream, be extravagant with your desires. If you can dream it, you can make it happen.

Your dream can be as outrageous as you want, as supposedly unattainable as you can imagine. Have you always wanted to be an astronaut? An actor? A musician? A writer? A chef? A fashion stylist? A doctor? A farmer? Maybe it's a marine biologist. A furniture maker. An underwater archaeologist. A hairstylist. A college professor. Maybe your dream isn't a profession but rather a place you want to reach, an achievement you want to conquer. Own your own Benz. Own a big ol' home with five bedrooms and a swimming pool. Live in New York City. Live in the country. Live in another country. Maybe it's to earn a Nobel Prize. Or win the Kentucky Derby. Or the World Cup.

No dream is too crazy or too out there. The important thing is for you to dream it, and then let it live. Give it life by letting yourself say it, own it, chase it. In this book, we're going to talk a lot about dreams and visualizing what your life as a Future Millionaire might look like, and I don't want you to get too bogged down right now by trying to imagine how you'll actually make your dream happen. Never worry about the *how* when it's time to dream. We'll get to that how, but for right now, I just want you to dream. Think about what your truest heart wants for your life. What would you wish for if you had a magic wand?

Now make it real. Say it out loud. Say it on social media, if you feel bold enough. Or just say it to a friend, or a bunch of friends. Write it out and review it often. The key is to lock it down somewhere outside your own brain. This makes it stick. Otherwise, it's too easy to give yourself an out later on (especially when the going gets tough), to "come back to your senses" and dismiss the dream as impossible, to convince yourself that it was a stupid idea after all. Or worse, to let someone else crush your dream for you. **Don't let anyone convince you that your dream is impossible.** Take concrete action and nail that dream down, or else your doubts and fears will get the upper hand.

TRY IT: What is your biggest dream? I want you to write your dream down in as much detail as you can. What do you do with your time? How do you earn your money? Where do you live, and who are you hanging out with?

If you'd like a little help creating your detailed dream, download the Million Dollar Dream worksheet at futuremillionaire.me.

Once you have written down your Million Dollar Dream, tell a friend. Post it on social media. Write it down for only you to see. Whatever works for you. Just give it life somewhere outside your own head. Go ahead, do it now.

Your Million Dollar Why

After you have figured out your big dream, the next step is to ask yourself: Why? Why is it important to me to make a million dollars? What will having that money do for me? How will it allow me to change my life, my family's life, and the world? How will it enable me to have a positive impact? Why THIS dream?

Think about why you want to make money. If it's just to have enough cash to buy something you want, that's cool, but it may not be enough to keep you out on the metaphorical road to riches when you hit a nasty thunderstorm or your tire goes flat. Once you get that shiny new thing you want so bad, or once its novelty has worn off, will you get back out on the road? Most people who achieve real wealth have a deeper reason that keeps them going. I think of this as a Million Dollar Why.

Million Dollar Why: *(noun)* The drive and motivation behind your Million Dollar Dream. It's why this dream is important to you, and it may also help you identify what is going to be possible when this dream comes true, i.e., your purpose.

The reason you need to figure out your Million Dollar Why is because when the going gets tough, your why will keep you going. It's easy enough to think, *I want to be wealthy.* Don't we all, Sis! But just *wanting* isn't enough to equal *getting.* It's like deciding to take a trip. Let's say we wanna go to Moolah Town. That's all fine and good, but just thinking, *Hey, a road trip might be nice* isn't gonna get you out of the driveway. *Why* do you want to take that trip? That's the thing that will get you to pack your bags, grab a map, and actually head out the door. Dreams require effort. Our Why reminds us of our motivations to do the hard work of making it happen.

For me and for many of the other millionaires I know, that Why is a desire to provide a life we didn't have as kids. We want to take care of our families, to give back to loved ones who scraped and sacrificed for us. I've already described my own experiences with the stress of not having enough money, and as a young person I promised myself a better future.

My friend Corey Arvinger, the founder and CEO of an apparel company called Support Black Colleges, started his company in college, but it wasn't his first stint as an entrepreneur. Corey saw his single mother working multiple jobs to pay the bills and put food on the table, and he didn't feel right using her hard-earned money for the things he wanted as a kid. So to get the pocket money he wanted, he started selling homemade popsicles, and later he sold snacks to the kids at school. If you want to be wealthy to support your family and earn your way out of the stress and fear of poverty, that's a pretty a damn good Why.

What's your Why? It's okay if you've got your heart set on a nice car or a pricey house and that's what's pushing you to make your money. But your Million Dollar Why needs to push you in the tough times too, the times when people doubt you, or you don't get the loan you were counting on, or you're in the sacrifice phase of your work life and you start to doubt that real cash will ever see the inside of your wallet. Working toward a single object or a purchase may not keep you going if things start getting a little too real. You may talk yourself out of doing the hard work by rationalizing that it's easier just to live without that thing.

A Million Dollar Why gets at the heart of who you want to become. Maybe you're someone who's determined not to put her family through the same hardships she witnessed, or someone who wants to put money into—not take it out of—the pockets of his hard-working mama. Or someone who wants to be fairly compensated for their own amazing ideas and hard work. Or someone who wants to build wealth to lift up herself *and* her community.

TRY IT: Think about your Million Dollar Why. Write it down somewhere so you can refer to it and stay focused, helping you never lose sight of what has put you on the road and is driving you to become a Future Millionaire.

I'd like to introduce you to someone who had a really strong Million Dollar Why. She is someone who wanted a better life for herself and for her entire community. She followed her dream despite all the odds against her and she did, in fact, make her life and the life of Black Americans better. This Million Dollar Dreamer is Madam C. J. Walker.

Maybe you've already heard about her, but if not, she was the G.O.A.T. dreamer: the nation's first female self-made millionaire, *and* a Black woman living her truth in late 1800s America. Many of us face more than our fair share of obstacles today that make it harder for us to get ahead, but Madam C. J. was born in 1867, just five years after the Emancipation Proclamation. She was the only member of her family not born into slavery. Madam Walker—or Sarah, as she was named—grew up amid rampant racial violence during Reconstruction, in a world that constantly insisted that a Black person had no worth. Schools were burned to the ground, Black people were murdered indiscriminately. For young Sarah, prosperity must have seemed impossible. Her parents died when she was just seven. She grew up with her older sister and worked the cotton fields of the Deep South, then fled her sister's abusive husband and married at age fourteen. Her husband died several years later and Sarah, by then a young mother, worked as a washerwoman to support herself and her daughter.

But then she met a Black entrepreneur named Annie Malone. Annie sold haircare treatments, and she brought Sarah on as a salesperson. At first, Sarah just sold the products on the side, to supplement her domestic work. But this exposure to entrepreneurship made her want to build her own business. Eventually, Sarah developed her own haircare products. She understood the importance of marketing and worked hard traveling around the country to get the word out about her business. Soon, she had a steady stream of clients and a regular income.

When she married a newspaper man named Mr. Walker in 1906, she took on the name Madam C. J. Walker. That same year, she turned her haircare products into a full-fledged business: The Madam C. J. Walker Manufacturing Company. From there, she built her business into a national enterprise. She traveled the country promoting her products, and trained other Black women to sell them, paying forward the opportunity she'd been given and offering financial stability and economic mobility to Black women across the country. At a time when the majority of Black women were working as domestic servants earning $100 to $240 a year, Madam C. J. Walker was making multitudes more than that. She made $3,652 her first year alone, equivalent to roughly $104,000 today. She went on to build factories to manufacture her products, a salon, and a training school; in the space of just sixteen years, she became a millionaire. She also trained more than twenty thousand Black women, who excelled in sales and became wealthy themselves. In addition to providing financial opportunity, she taught her employees to give back and to use their wealth to help their communities and to wield political power.

Little about Madam C. J. Walker's upbringing pointed to opportunity and privilege. In fact, she had only three months of formal education. But despite the racism, sexism, violence, and lack of opportunities, she found a way to flourish.

I tell you this because Madam C. J. Walker is still a role model for how to thrive despite your current circumstances. You don't need to have a perfect childhood, an Ivy League education, or wealthy connections to pursue the life you imagine for yourself. You just need to give yourself the permission to dream, and then the courage to chase after it.

Now that we're all hyped by Madam C. J., let's start making our own dreams come true!

Chapter Summary

- In order to become a millionaire, you have to allow yourself to dream like a millionaire.
- Despite the circumstances you may have been born into, or the systemic racism, sexism, homophobia, ableism, and other systemic prejudices that may exist in your life, you deserve and are capable of building wealth.
- Identifying your Million Dollar Dream is the first step to becoming a millionaire.
- Achieving your dream becomes easier when you identify your Million Dollar Why—the deeper, underlying reason why you want to build wealth.
- Madam C. J. Walker, America's first self-made female millionaire, is a reminder that no matter your circumstances, building wealth is possible.

CHAPTER 2

Think Like a Millionaire

In order to make your Million Dollar Dream happen, you need to think like a millionaire. Your thinking can be a springboard for untold success, or it can be where your dreams end before they even begin. Believe it or not, it all hinges on your thoughts.

So how do millionaires think?

According to Tom Corely—the author of the book *Rich Habits,* who spent five years studying and interviewing 233 millionaires to determine their habits and how they think—millionaires think positively, they believe in their ability to improve, they refuse to quit on their dreams (i.e., they are resilient), they are solution-oriented, and they believe they will find a way to solve their problems. Millionaires have a clear goal (a Million Dollar Dream, if you will). They know what they want, and they have a plan to get there. They have a gratitude practice, where they are reflecting on all that they have to be grateful for on a daily basis. They are willing to learn from their mistakes, and they set up systems and habits in their life to help them win. Most of all, millionaires are patient. They may want their dream today, but they understand that success takes time to unfold, and they are willing to continue to show up and be consistent until it happens.[1]

So how do you begin to adopt a millionaire's mindset? You start with your current thoughts.

Million Dollar Thought: *(noun)* Thoughts that make you feel powerful; thoughts that remind you that you are smart, resourceful, and capable of anything you want to achieve.

Many of us don't even realize that we have a negative tape recorder playing in our heads all day with the same negative thoughts. Your tape recorder may be playing thoughts like, *You're so dumb, you're so ugly, you're such a loser, no one likes you.* As you can see, your tape recorder is a mean bully, and we need to shut it off. No, let's go further. We need to fling that tape recorder across the park so it breaks into a thousand pieces, never to be heard from again! (That's how detrimental it is to your happiness and future.) But how do you do that with your metaphorical tape recorder? There is a way! It's called thought work.

Growing up, I had a few role models for wealth—two of my aunts lived financially comfortable lives and helped take care of me. They showed me how having money allowed you to live a life with more ease, free from the stress of financial crises. When I was a teenager, I babysat a young girl whose family had a fancy house on a tree-lined street and all the snacks a person could ever want. (So many frozen pizza bagels and Pop-Tarts, the kinds of things our family couldn't afford.) They were always super generous with me, and they showed me that people could be rich and still be kind. And of course, I saw how hard my own parents worked.

So I did have a sense that it was possible for someone like me to make money and live comfortably. They also showed me different ways of being wealthy. You could be no nonsense and take no crap, like my aunties; you could be the very personification of kindness; or you could be both at the same time.

But the years of financial struggles that my parents, sister, and I experienced made me believe that even if I did achieve financial success, it could all go away. I feared that I might be able to have money for a time, but I would never be able to count on it long-term.

I made my first million when I was thirty-five years old—which may sound young, but it actually took me longer than it might have otherwise, because I had no mentors, no one advising me, and I was carrying all that fear around. I still carry that fear of financial struggle. The difference now is, when those fears start telling me sad tales of despair, I engage in thought work. This is how I've developed a millionaire's mind.

Thought Work

Thought work involves taking conscious, intentional steps to override the deeply ingrained stories we tell ourselves that tear us down and steal our confidence. So when your brain starts up with its negative thoughts, you can reconsider them from a different perspective and tell yourself a new story.

When my brain tries to tell me I could lose everything I've worked so hard for, I literally tell myself, "That's just a story my mind is telling me. It has no power over me unless I let it. It's a thought, not a reality."

That's a crucial thing to remember about the negative stories we tell ourselves: *they're just thoughts*. They aren't true unless we believe them and act on them (therefore making them come true). Which is great news! It means that **you can choose to believe something different**.

For me, I can look at the facts of my experience and remind myself that, actually, I make smart decisions about money. I can believe in my ability to use my knowledge and experiences to keep making those smart decisions. Even if I make a big mistake or something forces me to lose my money, I can choose to believe that my skills will get me right back on my feet. My fear about losing it all is just a thought. It is not reality.

We tell ourselves these kinds of thoughts every day. Do any of these sound familiar?

- Ugh, I look hideous.
- God, I'm so stupid. What I just did was so stupid.
- I'm never going to get that raise.
- I'm never going to look like *that*.
- No wonder that didn't work out for me. I'm such an idiot.

It's crazy when you think about it! Why are we so mean to ourselves??

Our cruel thoughts can be very sneaky, and they slip in and ambush us in tons of creative and hurtful ways.

So how do we tell these thoughts to shut up? Thought work. The key is to remember that **you have control over your thoughts**. Often, our negative thoughts arise from messages we learn in our community, from our fractured culture, or from listening to our families or friends. We can't make negative thoughts disappear completely, but we also don't have to give them power. You're the boss. Just because you think these thoughts doesn't mean they're true.

Thought work involves a few steps.

STEP 1: Notice the thought. I like to think of this as a version of I Spy. As in, *I spy . . . my critical mind trying to get judgy on me.* What you want to do is step outside of yourself as a spectator and notice what thoughts are running through your head. When you notice a negative thought that is not serving you (i.e., it makes you feel bad about yourself), write it down.

STEP 2: Question the thought. Ask yourself a series of questions about this particular thought. Remember, you're a spy and you're going to use your spy skills to interrogate this thought. Ask yourself:

- Is this thought helpful? Does it make you feel good or terrible? If it makes you feel good, great! That means it's serving you. If it gives you negative feelings, move on to the next question.
- Is this thought true? Really think about this one. Would this thought hold up in a court of law? Is it a fact? For example, is it a fact that "you're so stupid"? Or is that just a judgy comment that isn't really rooted in fact? If you think, *Actually, no, I am not so stupid. I am just being mean to myself; I don't truly believe that I am stupid*, then maybe your work here is done. However, if there is something in the back of your mind saying, *To be honest, I think it's true—I am stupid*, then move on to the next step.

STEP 3: Look for evidence of the opposite of what your negative thought is telling you. If the thought is *I'm so stupid*, what evidence do you have to prove you aren't stupid? Look for facts from your real life that prove this thought wrong. Literally sit down and write a list of evidence that this thought has it totally wrong. Your list might include things like: I got an A in Biology and that's a really hard class; I figured out how to fix that customer service problem at work and my boss was really proud of me; I helped my mom organize the garage, figured out where to donate old stuff, and created a new organizational system to keep things neat going forward . . . only a smart person could do that. *Boom!* You've just created brand-new neuropathways in your brain. The next time the thought *I'm so stupid* pops into your brain, instead of believing it, you'll think of all this evidence that shows it's just not true.

STEP 4: Reframe this negative thought. Now that we have proven that this thought is false, it's time to come up with a reframe. When the thought *I'm so stupid* pops into your brain, you'll say to yourself, "That's just not true," and then replace it with a better, truer thought. For example, if you make a mistake, instead of thinking *I'm so stupid*, you can reframe that thought to *I made a mistake and it doesn't feel good, but at least now I know what not to do.*

Congrats! You just did thought work! The good news is that thought work is easy and anyone can do it. The bad news is it's not a one and done fix. Thought work is a constant practice. However, if you take the time to go through this process with your most repetitive negative thoughts, over time you will notice those thoughts go away almost completely. Suddenly the Mean Girl (or Boy or Person) in your head has stopped talking and the thoughts you are regularly having are mostly positive.

Here is a list of common negative thoughts and reframes that you can use.

ZERO DOLLAR THOUGHT	MILLION DOLLAR THOUGHT
Ugh, I look hideous. I'm never going to look like *that*.	First, notice the thought. *Ah, there you are again, my judgy nemesis. I see you, up to your old tricks again.* Question the thought: Is it helpful to tell yourself these things? Are they true? (The answer is almost always a hell no.) Are you conveniently ignoring the fact that you just got caught in a big ol' storm? Or that you don't spill coffee down your shirt every single day, and this just happens to be one of those

	days? Are you forgetting about all those days when you look fire? Bring in the subs! A reconsidered thought: *This is just a thought. It's not reality. I may be more tired than usual today, but I'll get to bed earlier tonight and feel fresher tomorrow.* Or, *I don't have to look like that to love how I look.*
Why did I just say that? I'm so stupid. No wonder that didn't work out. I'm such an idiot.	Notice the thought. Question the thought. Is this helpful? Is it true? Reframed: *That didn't work out the way I intended it to, but it doesn't mean anything about my intelligence. Everybody stumbles over their words and actions sometimes. I don't need to dwell on it or beat myself up. I'm just going to acknowledge my misstep and move on.*
I'm never going to get that raise.	Notice the thought. Question the thought. Reframed: *Here are all the reasons why I've earned a raise. I work hard and I deserve to be compensated for my efforts. I'll take these examples to my boss, but if I don't get the raise, it isn't proof that I don't deserve it.*

Our negative thoughts don't predict the future. They aren't inevitable.

A lot of the punch of a negative thought comes from responding to a single, specific incident with broad generalizations about ourselves, especially using statements that attack our self-worth. To misspeak or have a bad hair day doesn't mean we're stupid or a mess. It's just a sign of our humanness. We're all flawed! Don't give it more power than that. We tend to be so much kinder to others than we are to ourselves. Would you talk like this to your mother or your best friend? Don't be a bully, especially to yourself! Practice kindness toward yourself.

It bears repeating that just doing this once or twice isn't going to magically make these thoughts disappear. They've probably taken years to fully set up shop in your brain, and taking away their power requires practicing these steps over and over again, whenever the thought pops up, until the negative thoughts aren't your brain's first response to a triggering situation. Don't get discouraged and don't beat yourself up if they keep coming back. Imagine the thoughts like little beasties in a game of Whack-a-Mole, and just keep whomping them on the head when they appear. Soon enough, they'll get the message: you're in charge here.

TRY IT: What are some negative thoughts you find yourself thinking regularly? If you're not sure, try paying attention over the next couple of days to the things you tell yourself. Write them down and then practice doing thought work on them. When the thoughts come up the next time, acknowledge them, then reconsider them from your new, more positive perspective. Get into the habit of practicing thought work whenever you find yourself drifting toward the negative.

Use the Million Dollar Thoughts worksheet to practice. You can download it at futuremillionaire.me.

Telling Ourselves New Stories

Another aspect of thought work involves telling ourselves different stories. Our brain isn't our enemy, but sometimes it needs to be nudged toward working *for* us, not against us. So part of the *work* of thought work is rewriting the stories that cause us harm.

Why stories? Because we're naturally wired to seek them; we understand things about the world and our lives through stories. But when those stories make us believe negative, damaging things about ourselves, it's time to try something different. There's a famous quote that says that madness is doing the same thing and expecting a different result. If you want your circumstances to be different, if you want to improve something about your life, you may have to try a different approach than what you've been doing. We can use our storytelling instinct to tell ourselves stories that inspire us, that motivate us, that help us achieve our goals.

Here are a few common negative stories people have about money, and guidance for telling yourself a different, better story. If you can learn to change your negative thoughts about money, results will follow.

PEOPLE LIKE ME DON'T MAKE A LOT OF MONEY. As we discussed earlier, think about what might have made you believe you're unworthy in the first place. What negative influences have been whispering in your ear? A family member, a teacher, the big mouths in our culture who think they know what you're capable of or know who is "allowed" to make money? Stop listening to them and tell yourself a new story. For starters, think about what you've been through in your life. What challenges have you faced? What difficulties have you survived? Are there times you've had to stand up for yourself? These can be big or small. Nothing you've been through is insignificant.

Maybe it's something huge like a difficult move or the death of a loved one, or maybe it's something more personal, like a friend's betrayal or an opportunity that didn't go your way. All the difficulties we experience shape us and make us stronger. Even if you didn't feel tough at the time, the things you've endured, the obstacles you've overcome are proof of how strong you really are. You did it, and you're still here. You're one Big, Beautiful Ball of Strength.

So what kind of people are you thinking of when you think that people "like you" can't make a lot of money? Strong people? Butt-kicking people who survive the challenges that come their way? People who make mistakes and learn from them, then come out stronger? Those kinds of people?!? In my mind, you're *exactly* the kind of person who can make a lot of money.

Also, you can tell a different story by looking to financial role models. Is there somebody out there crushing it and living your dream already? You don't have to know them personally. Maybe it's somebody you follow on TikTok. Maybe it's somebody who's made it big doing something you're passionate about too. Research how they got to where they are. Look at their bio on their website, check out their social media. Consider reaching out by email or DM, if you can, and ask them directly. There are people "like you" making bank right now. Look to them for inspiration and to tell yourself a new story. They're no different than you, except that they believed they could do it and they put in the work. They did it, and so can you! *This* is the story you should be telling yourself. Not that people "like you" can't make a lot of money, but that you're exactly the kind of person who *can* make a lot of money.

You have to work really hard to make money. You've probably grown up watching the people around you work really hard. Maybe you've seen your parents hustle and struggle and wear themselves out, and all the while they still don't have a lot of money to show for all their effort. Maybe the stress and hard work even took a toll on their bodies and spirits. All these things may make you feel like chasing money isn't worth it.

Yes, there is effort involved in making money, but it doesn't have to be body- and soul-crushing. We'll get into the specifics in part two of this book, but there are ways to work smarter, not harder, to get wealthy. People who are good at making money know that it's almost impossible to make bank just from a paycheck alone. Wealth is often built through buying assets (stocks and real estate are two examples). These assets increase in value over time. When you go to sell that asset, you cash in on that increase in value, and your bank account grows without you having to break a sweat. We'll dig more into this and explore some other avenues in part two, but don't keep yourself completely out of the game when there are many ways to play.

I'm just not good with money. Let's clear this up right now: Nobody is "good" or "bad" with money from birth. Money skills are something you have to learn. And anyone can be taught. Even that little old lady at the coffee shop, adding up the tip on her fingers.

This is one of the ways our stories can hold us back. Because we sometimes overlook important information that might change the story's meaning. Some people grow up having conversations about money from a young age, for example. So they may be comfortable with the language of stocks and bonds the way some people grow up learning both English and Korean, because it's part of the environment they're raised in. But it's not your fault if that's not you. Your situation isn't hopeless. That wasn't my experience either, but look at me now. That's why we're here. I learned how to do the work to change my stories, and you can too. Let's rewrite yours today: your money game is about to level up.

It's completely okay if you've believed any of these myths yourself.

Recognizing these thoughts in yourself and learning to tell yourself new stories is growth. You're thinking like a millionaire already! The real mistake is not trying to change these thoughts, now that you understand how they might be holding you back.

Besides money myths, how else might your stories be holding you back?

Maybe you believe you can't be a leader in one of your school clubs because the people who tend to be the leaders are those folks who also tend to be the talkers. Not being a talker doesn't mean you can't be a leader. And telling yourself that it does may actually be preventing you from pursuing something you might be really good at. In fact, some of the best leaders are those who know when to stay quiet and listen to others before they act.

By telling yourself you can't be ____________ (fill in the blank) because you think you lack some quality that seems vital to the job, you're just selling yourself short and ignoring the skills you do have to offer. As with the money myths, this is just a story your brain is telling you. It's not an actual fact that you can't be a leader. Your new story might look like this: *I can be a leader precisely* because *I bring a different set of skills that this group would really benefit from. I want to get involved, and I have something unique and important to offer.*

Maybe you think you can't go to college, that you're not "college material," but you have a passion for science and think you'd love having a career in a science field. Maybe no one in your family has gone to college, so you don't have the role models to show you how to go about it. Your brain considers that information and decides college must not be an option for you either.

Well guess what, Brain, that's just a story, not actual fact, and it's not a very good one either. A better story is this: *I love science, I'm good at science, and I can find a way to go to college to study it. It may take more work on my part, and I may need to ask for help from guidance counselors and teachers, but I* am *college material. And I'll be a role model for the family members who come after me.*

When you replace your old stories with ones that lift you up and encourage you to reach for what you want, you feel better. You feel motivated and inspired. These things feel good—a whole lot better than when you're tearing yourself down. And you deserve to feel good. When you do, you're much more likely to make choices that will help keep those good feelings coming.

Negative thoughts are a learned habit, but so are positive thoughts. You can choose to think more affirming thoughts. As I said, it takes practice and repetition—think of it as a muscle you have to exercise regularly—but the more you stop the negative thoughts in their tracks, question them, and replace them with positive ones, the easier and more automatic the habit becomes.

Note: None of this is meant to say that you must be cheerful and bubbly all the time, or that you need to fake positivity. Feelings like sadness, anger, and frustration are completely normal and okay. (I'm no bubbly ray of sunshine all the time myself. I keep it real and, yep, I can be kind of ornery. But thought work makes a huge difference.) This is about breaking the thought habits that keep you stuck, that keep you doubting yourself, and that keep you from dreaming your Million Dollar Dreams.

Here are some common money-related thoughts that hold people back.

Zero Dollar Thought	Million Dollar Thought
The system is rigged.	Yes, the world can be unkind and unfair, but I can play the game on my own terms and win. I'm going to be a millionaire to make the world a better place.
I'll never pay off these student loans.	I am capable of changing my situation. There are resources and strategies for paying off loans, and there are people who can help me figure out a plan. I'm in control of my actions, and I can take steps to deal with this.
I feel stuck and I don't even know where to start.	I'm not stuck at all. Starting is the hardest part, and by asking questions and reading this book, I'm showing up for myself.
The thing I really want to do isn't something that makes a lot of money.	There are an infinite number of ways to make money, and doing what brings me joy and suits my interests can also make me money. I have skills to offer, and I have the determination to use them to make money.
The only rich people I've ever encountered are jerks. Who wants to turn into that? Better to just stay broke.	Poor and rich people can be jerks, and poor and rich people can be kind. If I'm a jerk, it's not money's fault. I'm in control of my behavior and the kind of person I want to be.

TRY IT: If any of these Zero Dollar Thoughts sound familiar to you, it's time to start thinking like a millionaire. Practice replacing broke thoughts with better ones. There's no time like the present to start trying on your new Million Dollar Thoughts.

Use the Million Dollar Thoughts worksheet to practice. You can download it at futuremillionaire.me.

Now that we've talked about what thought work is, let's talk about what thought work isn't. As important and life-changing as thought work can be, it doesn't solve all the world's problems, of course. No amount of thought work can change your identity group, nor should it. If you are a person of color, if you are LGBTQIA+, if you are part of any other marginalized group, thought work can't undo the discrimination you may experience as you move through the world. And other people's meanness isn't your fault. There is nothing wrong with you when harmful treatment makes you feel angry or sad, and you do not need to do thought work to feel less hurt by it. How thought work can come into play here is to learn how to revise the impact the stories may have, to help you choose a more empowering response.

For example, you might think, *Racism is so baked into the system that I'll never be able to get ahead*. But while the first fact is true, you do have control over your own actions and behavior. The first fact doesn't cancel out the second.

So thought work in this case might involve reframing your thoughts to something that helps inspire you to action, rather than to shut down: *Because of racism, I must build wealth. Yes, racism and systemic discrimination infect many systems in America. And it's exactly because of that fact that I will make it a priority to get ahead and build wealth, so I can show others in my community that it's possible for them too.*

As with many of the other Million Dollar Thoughts, this reframed thought takes strength from the power of your own actions. You may not be able to control *what* happens in the world, or even in your community, and your emotions in response to those events are completely valid. But you do get to choose how you respond to those events. I have experienced racism and sexism in my own life, and you better believe it has made me angry and sad. But it doesn't stop me. I also choose to believe in my ability to build wealth in spite of racism, sexism, and systemic oppression. You get to choose your response to what is happening in the world too.

When you think positively, you are thinking like a millionaire. The positivity in your head will help you believe in yourself and your ability to accomplish your Million Dollar Dream. If you believe you can do it, you'll take the action to make it happen. If you don't believe, it will be difficult to take any action. Practice thought work and reframe the negative stories you are telling yourself every day to give yourself the best chance at achieving your Million Dollar Dream. And, even more exciting than that, you'll be happier and just feel better too. That's worth a million dollars right there!

Chapter Summary

- In order to become a millionaire, you have to start thinking like a millionaire.
- Thought work, the practice of regularly evaluating your thoughts and reframing your negative thoughts, can help you begin to think like a millionaire.
- Replace the common negative stories in your mind—like *People like me don't make a lot of money*, *you have to work really hard to make money*, and *I'm just not good with money*—with stories that place you back in your power.
- Thought work is a powerful practice but it should not be used to invalidate your experience as a systemically marginalized person. You can't think racism away.
- Despite this, focusing on positivity and possibility will spur you to take action toward your Million Dollar Dream.

CHAPTER 3

Decide Like a Millionaire

While taking a class on cosmetic formulation in college, Marlene realized all the big beauty brands were selling makeup that wasn't necessarily good for your skin. This bothered her, and she wanted to solve the problem by creating makeup that was actually so beneficial for your skin it would be considered skin care. After completing her associate's degree in beauty marketing and product development, Marlene was ready to develop her own beauty product: tinted skin care that doesn't just look good but is good.

"Everyone told me it would be impossible to start a beauty brand of this scale, let alone create a whole new entire category of product," says Marlene. Despite the naysayers and potentially large barriers to entry, Marlene persisted. More importantly, she decided. Marlene made a Million Dollar Decision that she was going to address this issue in the marketplace by creating sustainable, ethical, inclusive tinted skin care. Once that decision was made, and Marlene's actions followed, opportunity began flowing her way.

Marlene started working on Blancos Beauty in 2020 while continuing her education in business management. She joined forces with her best friend, with whom she had run a lemonade stand at just eight years old. Together, they were able to accumulate the initial startup capital with no outside investors and used preorder sales from their community to continue funding the business. She also recruited help from contacts she had made at a previous job at a large marketing firm. At the firm, Marlene had fostered relationships with influencers and other folks who were able to help her spread the word when she launched Blancos. (In chapter 8, we'll discuss how jobs can be a stepping stone toward your Million Dollar Dream by giving you the skills, resources, and contacts you need to make it happen.)

After four years of working on the business and formulating the products, Blancos Beauty officially launched in February 2024. Blancos Beauty blends natural pigments and luxurious botanicals to create tinted skin care products that are FDA approved as skin care, just as Marlene had envisioned (nay, decided!). *Forbes* featured Blancos Beauty Skin Soufflé on its list of Best New Skincare for 2024, and PopSugar listed Blancos Beauty Flush as a Beauty Launch Our Editors Can't Get Enough Of.

Just five months after launch, Blancos Beauty had generated $450,000 in revenue, allowing Marlene and her business partner to fully recover their initial investment and turn a six-figure profit. Additionally, the company scored a featured placement in a well-known retailer. Marlene says, "Blancos was born from a dream, and every day I pinch myself that my dream became a reality."

So how can you turn your Million Dollar Dream into reality? Just decide.

Million Dollar Decisions vs. Zero Dollar Decisions

Your thoughts go hand in hand with the actions you take. That's just basic science: We all make decisions based on the thought processes in our heads that tell us, *Do this. Don't do that.* So when you start shifting negative and defeating thoughts into positive, empowering ones, you find that positive, empowering decisions will follow.

But when you're young, many decisions have been made for you most of your life—whether you liked them or not. As a result, you may not have had much experience taking charge of your own actions, and you may have developed habits that could make it harder to achieve your financial goals.

Maybe you haven't had the opportunity to learn how to save up for a big purchase, for example. You've always just spent whatever money comes your way as soon as you get it. Part of growing up and becoming independent is learning to recognize the habits that may be holding you back, so you can learn to make better, wiser decisions. One of the great things about being young is that young people are wonderfully open to learning and trying new things. You're not stubborn and set in your ways; you're hyped up and ready for bigger and better things!

So let's discuss what wise decisions look like. Similar to thought work, they require that you recognize which habits and decisions are productive and which ones are holding you back. Far too often, we make decisions that don't move us closer to our dream. In fact, they might even get in our way. These decisions are often the end result of the kinds of harmful thought patterns that thought work aims to change. We *think* we're making smart decisions, when really we're not doing ourselves any favors.

I think of these as either Million Dollar Decisions or Zero Dollar Decisions. Million Dollar Decisions are smart, intentional; they show that you've got your mindset straight, and you know your worth.

A Million Dollar Decision is one that:

- frees up your time and energy so you can devote them to the things that move you toward your goals
- reduces the demands on your mental space
- builds you up and makes you feel strong, independent, and able to make the choices you *want* to make in your life
- opens up opportunities

A Zero Dollar Decision is one that holds you back. It's one that:

- saps your time, drains your energy, and robs you of the resources to pursue your goals
- taxes your mental mojo
- knocks you down and makes you feel vulnerable, dependent, stuck
- closes doors, shuts down opportunities, and leaves you with fewer, not more, choices

Every decision you make in life, every action you take, is leading you somewhere. Even if it's just sitting in your room scrolling through Instagram. Or out causing mischief with your friends. Or committing to launching a business like Marlene did. Every action is a decision you've made that is moving you forward (or not). The question is, are you on a path that's bringing you closer to your dream, or taking you farther away? Consider these examples:

ZERO DOLLAR DECISIONS	MILLION DOLLAR DECISIONS
You let your friend borrow the new Air Force Ones you worked hard to buy, and they were predictably returned scuffed and muddy. You are really upset.	Your friend asks to borrow your new Air Force Ones. You kindly say no. You explain that those shoes represent weeks of hard work, and that you are not open to sharing them. Your friend is disappointed, but you are proud of yourself for being honest and protecting your stuff.
Your teacher insists that the class work on group projects, but you end up doing all the work while the rest of the group collects the good grade.	You work with the group to set clear guidelines about who will be responsible for which part of the project, and you make it clear that you will only be doing your share of the work. Then you make sure your teacher understands the division of labor once the project is turned in, so she knows who pulled their weight.
Your cousin knows you're great with hair, so she brags about you to her friends, who want in on your skills—for free. You don't love it, but you figure the positive word of mouth is payment enough.	You thank your cousin for the referrals but explain that hairstyling is part of how you're paying for school, and you will not be able to do all her friends' hair for free. But you agree to give her a free do for every three new customers she refers to you.
You want to get your CPR certification to improve your job prospects as a babysitter, but the course costs money you don't have, so you keep accepting less than you could be making instead of being able to increase your rates.	You recognize that taking the course is an investment in yourself, so you take on extra babysitting gigs and save until you can pay for the course, then promptly increase your rates once certified.

You've just graduated from college, you have a scary amount of debt, and you take the first (low-paying) job offer you get just to start bringing in a paycheck.	You research salaries in your chosen field and go into your job interview knowing what you should expect to make in an entry-level position. You know your worth, and you come to the interview prepared to show what you bring to the position and why you should get paid an above-market salary.
Your friends ask you to attend a party on a weeknight. You know you want to get up early and get a head start on an important project. You go anyway, and the next morning you wake up late and are tired all day. You make no progress on your important project and you're mad at yourself.	Your friends ask you to attend a party on a weeknight. You say no thank you. You are bummed to miss out, but you also feel good about putting your priorities first. You wake up in the morning feeling fresh and make significant progress on your important project.

The thing to remember here is that no matter what decision you make, even if you do nothing at all, you're still making a choice. And those choices add up to where you are now; they add up to where you're going. If you're not satisfied with your life right now, start making different choices.

The logic behind a Zero Dollar Decision usually comes down to a couple of things. First, most of us want to be liked. So we may make a decision, like loaning a friend money, because we care about our friends and we want them to like us. Or maybe we're afraid to ask for a raise because we don't want to rock the boat at work. But to have the agency, power, and financial freedom that comes with wealth, we have to stop making decisions out of a desire to be liked or a fear of upsetting somebody. This doesn't mean you can't be kind. It doesn't mean you have to come in hot and take down everybody who gets in your way. It just means being firm about chasing your goals. It means making money decisions that serve *your* interests, that open up your opportunities, and that are made in confidence and with a belief in your skills and your worth.

Another reason we make Zero Dollar Decisions is that they may seem like the smarter play, until you really do the math. It may seem indulgent or selfish to spend some of your precious cash on new clothes or a training seminar. You're thinking, *That sounds great in theory, but I should be saving as much as I can right now.* But here's the secret: you're investing in yourself. This doesn't mean go crazy and make purchases that break the bank. This is about investing in small changes that affect your confidence and enable you to take steps toward your goals.

For example, if you want to work overseas in the future but you lack the language skills you need to get the kind of jobs you want, paying for a tutor or course that can help you learn a second language faster and more fluently is a smart investment in the future you want for yourself.

Notice how the idea of purchasing something that will make achieving your goals more likely makes you feel. Does it make you feel more abundant and like you are stepping into possibility? Or does it make you feel closed off and like your dream isn't possible? Spending money can be scary, but when you are doing so with a smart plan that you can follow through on, it's not just spending money, it's making a Million Dollar Decision.

Likewise, if you want to start a jewelry-making business on the side and you need to invest in tools and supplies in order to start making your first pieces, make a Million Dollar Decision and go for it! Sometimes setting up a money-making opportunity requires you to spend money. It's only a waste if you don't plan to follow through and use those tools to make jewelry you can sell.

This can be true for other things too: investing in a wardrobe for your new job, investing in drop-off laundry services so you have more time to work on your side hustle, investing in a gym membership so you start your day with an energizing workout. Yes, it's scary to spend money on something you aren't 100 percent sure will pay off. But things that make you feel good, that fire up your confidence, and that prepare you to bring your best self to your job are worth it. *You* are worth it.

Investing in yourself is a Million Dollar Decision, hard stop.

> **What's a Zero Dollar Decision you're making right now? How can you change it into a Million Dollar Decision? What's something you can do right now to invest in your Million Dollar Dream?**

The Formula for Making Million Dollar Decisions

Listen, I'm not naive—I know how challenging it can be to make Million Dollar Decisions when you're young, you need money, and you're busting your butt just trying to get by. And because you're young (and you're human), you won't make the best decision every time. That's how you learn, right? But your generation has already been through so much, and I want you to come out the other side of your struggles winning. You are strong, resilient, and you *are* going to win. You're here, right? So when you're evaluating a decision, remember the word WIN:

W IS FOR WANT. What do you *want* to do? Check in with your deepest, truest desires rather than going by what other people say you should want or should do. Maybe it's something society expects of you, or your parents, or your friends. Before you make a decision, consider whether you're being influenced by what you want or by what others expect. Are you considering taking a full-time job that doesn't excite you instead of trying to find a way to make that killer internship work? Is someone saying you shouldn't spend money on important tools you really need to do your dream job well? It's smart to seek others' opinions, but make sure your decision reflects something *you* really want.

I IS FOR INTENTION. Will this decision move you toward your intentions for the future? Do you have a clear sense of how this decision will move you forward toward your intended goals? Even if it may create a temporary setback—an upfront expense, for example, or an investment of time before you complete that important course—if you understand your *intention*, you will know when a decision serves your larger purpose. Taking the time to pursue that important internship may make your semester more hectic, but it could provide excellent experience and contacts that can really pay off later. Conversely, blowing off a learning opportunity so you don't miss out on an event with your friends may feel good in the short-term, but will you regret it later on? When you're intentional about how a decision can lead to greater gains down the road, you can feel better about any short-term sacrifices you may have to make, because you're playing the long game.

N IS FOR NOW. What will this decision require of you *now* to be successful? What action will you need to take to put the decision in motion and achieve the desired results? What work will you have to commit to make this a Million Dollar Decision? Making a decision work for you is so much easier when you also formulate a plan for implementing it. (More on plans soon!) No dithering, no stalling! Identify the first thing—or two or three—you will need to do to begin executing this decision. This may need to be broken into several smaller action steps. When you can see the way forward and are honest about your willingness to do what's required, decisions that seemed hard, or ones you might have been tempted to reject, are much less daunting.

TRY IT: How can you use the WIN Formula to start making Million Dollar Decisions? First, what do you really, truly want? Think carefully about your intention–what's the purpose? How will this decision move you closer to your Million Dollar Dream? And what can you do right now to get started? Write down your WIN so that you have these steps right in front of you. Voila! A Million Dollar Decision is practically inevitable.

Use the Million Dollar Decision worksheet to practice. You can download it at futuremillionaire.me.

Use this formula the next time you need to analyze a decision and determine what a Million Dollar Decision would look like for you. Remember that a Million Dollar Decision is one that nurtures your time and energy, that creates opportunity, that supports your mental space, and that makes you feel strong, making the choices *you* want for the life you want. Remember that there is no crystal ball and you cannot predict the future. The Million Dollar Decision formula is meant to help you make the best decision you can with the information and resources you have available to you right now. Boldly make decisions that get you what you want, move you toward your intended goals, and enable you to take action now. Only you know what a Million Dollar Decision is for you; your parents, your professors, and your friends can't make these decisions for you. This is an inside job. There's no right or wrong answer here, only what's right for you, right now, in this particular moment in time.

As with thought work, it takes practice to make Million Dollar Decisions and to break habits that lead to Zero Dollar Decisions. Don't be too hard on yourself when you make mistakes—you're learning here. But if you make a Zero Dollar Decision, try to take a step back and assess what underlying habit might have steered you off course. Did you make a decision in order to be liked? Did you decide to give in to a short-term temptation, like going out with your friends, instead of working on your CPR course training? When something got hard, did you find yourself slipping back into defeating self-talk and entertaining thoughts of quitting? We've all been there, and it's absolutely okay! But try to pinpoint what thoughts led to a Zero Dollar Decision so you can identify the negative thoughts that lead to negative decisions. The more attuned you are to how your thoughts affect your decisions, the more you can turn Zero Dollar Decisions into Million Dollar ones.

TRY IT: I recommend keeping a decision log; this is a diary where you list out the key decisions you make. At the end of each month, look back at what you wrote and think through some key decisions you made that month. The decisions you record can be big ones (like deciding to quit your job) and smaller ones (like deciding to return that impulse purchase you made recently). Don't try to track every decision, but list at least three to five decisions you made that month. Once you have some distance from those decisions, ask yourself: did this turn out to be a Million Dollar Decision or a Zero Dollar Decision? If it was a Zero Dollar Decision, what thinking led to that decision? If it was a Million Dollar Decision, what was the WIN analysis that led to that decision?

Doing this will help you to get better and better at making Million Dollar Decisions, which will in turn build your decision-making confidence.

Use the Million Dollar Decision Log to track your decisions. You can download it at futuremillionaire.me.

Practice is fundamental to achieving your dreams. Success occurs because of all the smaller steps and habits you build along the way. Recognizing the thoughts and decisions that don't serve you and regularly practicing how to nurture new ones that will—these are the keys to achieving success.

Chapter Summary

- To become a millionaire, you're going to have to make decisions like a millionaire.
- Million Dollar Decisions are ones that free up your time and energy; reduce the demands on your mental space; build you up and make you feel strong, independent, and able to make the choices you *want* to make in your life; and open up opportunities for you.
- Use the WIN Formula to make Million Dollar Decisions: *W* is for *Want* (what do you want for the future?), *I* is for *Intention* (will this decision move you toward your intentions for the future?) and *N* is for *Now* (what will this decision require of you now to be successful?).
- Keep a Million Dollar Decision Log to track your decisions and gain confidence in your decision-making.

CHAPTER 4

Set Boundaries Like a Millionaire

In ninth grade, I started my first business as a ghostwriter. I found myself taking a history class with a bunch of high school seniors. Most of them had either failed the class before or had just never gotten around to taking it. They all had senioritis and were so over school at that point. They just wanted to get this semester over with and graduate. I, on the other hand, was a great writer, highly motivated to make money, and ambitious. So I set up a ghostwriting business where I secretly wrote history papers for most of the seniors in the class. (Hey, I didn't say the business was ethical!)

It started with one student who saw I was always pulling As. He asked if I would be willing to write his history paper for him. I said yes—for a fee, of course—and my new ghostwriting business was born. Soon he told his friends, and before you knew it, I had several clients. This meant that every time a paper was assigned in that class, I had to write six different versions so the teacher wouldn't catch on: one for me and one for each of my customers. I charged $50 per paper.

Besides the obvious risk I was taking of being caught and suspended from school, I also made some other entrepreneurial mistakes:

- I was undercharging.
- I was making myself vulnerable, because somebody could try to blackmail me (by reporting me to the principal) to get out of paying.

- I was typing each paper on a typewriter—this was back in the dark ages before laptops were a common thing—so I had put myself in a very labor-intensive position.
- And I still had all my own schoolwork to do, so I was totally overextended and stressed-out.

In short, I was overworked, underpaid, putting myself at great risk, and dealing with major time management issues.

As you might guess, the ghostwriting gig was ultimately too unstable, so I moved on to a job at a pet store in Queens. I used to go there after school, and I loved it. At first, I would stock and organize the inventory, then I moved up to working the register. The other employees working the registers were quite a cast of characters. They were all older than me, but still young—seventeen, eighteen, twenty. After a while, I found out that they were skimming cash from the registers. All of them. It was like a heist movie.

I sort of understood why they were doing it—one of them was living on her own at only sixteen years old, others were trying to help support their families, and we were getting paid like $7 an hour—but when they kept offering to deal me in, I had to set a boundary. I told them I would not rat them out, but I wanted no part of it and to stop asking. I had learned from my previous ghostwriting business and vowed that I would never do anything shady to make money ever again. It wasn't worth the awful feelings and the stress of looking over my shoulder. I found another job and left the pet store as soon as I could. I honestly loved that job, but I didn't want to get caught up in what was going on there. And, of course, the owners eventually found out, and all my former coworkers got in trouble. Turns out they'd collectively stolen tens of thousands of dollars!

Why am I telling you this? Well, for one, it can be tempting to cut corners and take advantage of the opportunities that are right in front of you, even if they're questionable. After all, you've got a Million Dollar Dream, and it's easy to feel like it's going to take a looooong time to get there. Shortcuts can be very attractive. But I promise you, you don't have to do shady things to make money. Those kinds of decisions can follow you for the rest of your life. Trust your gut and protect your integrity. Don't make foolish decisions for the short-term. Make smart decisions for the long-term.

And if you've made mistakes in the past, don't beat yourself up. We're all human. We all make mistakes (I just confessed to the world I wrote my classmates' papers in high school—none of us is exempt from screwing up!). Learn from your mistakes, acknowledge how it made you feel (terrible!), and decide you won't try that kind of thing ever again.

But also don't be afraid to set boundaries with the people around you and with yourself. The cashiers at the pet store were my friends and I had compassion for the very real personal challenges they were experiencing, but also knew I needed to set a boundary to protect myself. That was more important than being liked or accepted by them. In fact, I would argue that setting boundaries is an absolutely essential step to becoming a millionaire. And that is why this chapter is devoted to teaching you Million Dollar Boundaries.

Not breaking the law is Boundary #1. (I hope that one's a no-brainer.) But other boundaries may not be as obvious. Think about the Zero Dollar Decisions we talked about in the last chapter. A lot of those are the result of not setting boundaries.

Do you always seem to be stuck loaning clothes or money or homework answers to a friend? You need to set boundaries.

Letting people talk you into doing things you know you don't want to do? You're gonna need some boundaries.

Are you surrounded by people who don't support you, or who don't share your Million Dollar Ambitions? You need to set boundaries.

Doing all the work in a group project while the rest of the group cruises to a grade *you* earned them? You need to set boundaries.

Letting friends take advantage of your talents without paying you for your time and effort? Yes, yes, and oh yes. BOUN-DA-RIES.

Why boundaries? As an ambitious person with a Million Dollar Dream, you need to decide what's acceptable to you in achieving your goals. As kind, caring people, we get pulled into other people's drama, and we put other people's requests before our own waaay too often. This takes away from your time, drains your energy and resources, and makes it harder to go after your own dreams.

As a young person, you might feel especially pressured to give in to other people's demands on your time and energy. You love your parents and your friends, you want your classmates to like you and consider you reliable, you want to be an active member of your community. But I'm here to tell you that it's also okay to say no sometimes. You don't have to constantly give away your power. The only way to achieve your Million Dollar Dream is to decide which demands on your time are acceptable and which aren't.

Boundaries are also important because you need to be able to protect yourself. I hope you have plenty of people in your life who also want to protect you, but the first person in line for that job is you. The other people in your life can't read your mind. If you don't tell them what's acceptable to you, how are they gonna know? The sooner you learn how to use your voice and advocate for yourself and your needs, the better.

If you take on an extra shift at your part-time job, something else has to give. Maybe you'll have less energy or less time to study for a big test, or you'll end up having to stay up late to get all your homework done. Is that a tradeoff you're willing to make? Maybe so, if it leads to a raise. But if it doesn't pay off, if you start to feel too drained by it with no upside, if you start to feel taken advantage of, it's time to set some boundaries.

Is it important to step away from your side hustle so your friend can talk about her boyfriend trouble? Maybe, the first couple of times. But if you've heard her sob story for the zillionth time and she's just using you for free therapy but not actually trying to fix anything, it's time to set some boundaries.

When you set a boundary, you are protecting your time, your energy, your ideas, and your hard work. Those resources are *yours*, for getting *you* closer to your dream. Protect them like the riches they are.

> **When you set a boundary, you are protecting your time, your energy, your ideas, and your hard work. Those resources are *yours*, for getting *you* closer to your dream. Protect them like the riches they are.**

What are you tolerating right now? What boundaries are being pushed? Are you letting your parents tell you you're a fool for thinking you can start your own business? Are your roommates playing loud music in your dorm room every night while you're trying to study? Are you postponing college or putting off taking the leadership course you're excited about because your significant other doesn't want things to change?

I don't want you to feel bad if any of these scenarios apply to you. They're all too common, especially for young people. Those around us may not have malicious intent, but most folks will take as much as you're willing to give, and when you're young, you may feel especially pressured to give more of yourself. Far too often, young people feel pressure to work extra (unpaid?!) hours to get ahead. Or to take on extra tasks that they may not be compensated for, or even get credit for, out of a desire to be seen as a "team player" or to show that they can handle responsibility. You're also more likely to be less firm with your boundaries when you're in a new environment—say, settling in at college or a new job, or moving to a new city—and you're trying to form new friendships or are in a new relationship.

This isn't to say that you shouldn't be flexible—it's great to take initiative, challenge yourself with new responsibilities, and be thoughtful about someone else's needs. But you can also be taken advantage of. To set Million Dollar Boundaries, you have to learn where your line is and then learn to draw it, clear as day, for those around you to see.

Million Dollar Boundary: *(noun)* A declaration to yourself and others (friends, family, boss, and so on) where you clearly state what you will do, and won't do, in a given situation.

The purpose of setting a Million Dollar Boundary is to establish reasonable limits, protect your energy and sanity, and therefore feel more joyful, more powerful, and more money-full. Million Dollar Boundaries help you become rich in money, joy, time, and peace.

Here are some of the resources you might need to protect:

Your Time: Your time has value. Your life is made up of the minutes that pass every day. So be intentional about how you spend it. This may mean not taking on labor that you aren't compensated for; not getting bogged down by tasks that someone else could do for you (and instead outsourcing the task, like laundry or grocery shopping, to a service for hire); not getting sucked into things that drain your time, like mindlessly scrolling through social media or bingeing episode after episode of *Love Is Blind* when you could be working on your side hustle. You can set healthy boundaries by blocking off time on your calendar for the things that are important to you—the things that will bring you closer to your goals and your dream.

YOUR EMOTIONS: Time to bring out the garlic and fend off the energy vampires! If somebody doesn't support you and your ambitions, tears you down and makes you feel small, or is in the habit of trauma dumping on you, they're sucking up your emotional energy and leaving less for you to put toward your Million Dollar Dream. Maybe the energy vampire is your online life—trying to make the Instagram version of you seem as fire as that influencer you admire or getting caught up in the cattiness that's rampant online. These can be just as emotionally draining as the people in your real life. Notice how certain people and activities make you feel; if your energy is low and negative feelings come up whenever you are around that person or doing that thing, it's probably time to shut it down.

TRY IT: Assess where you might need to set some Million Dollar Boundaries. Think about what areas of your life are exhausting or disappointing. Write down three to five things you're sick of doing or areas of your life where you've been settling for crumbs. Where are the time sucks? Who or what is draining your energy? What is drawing down your cash flow? Don't hold back here—we can't solve the problem if we don't identify it.

Use the Million Dollar Boundaries worksheet for help with this exercise. You can download it at futuremillionaire.me.

YOUR MONEY: You're trying to make bank, not be a bank. Think carefully about where you're letting your money go. Loaning money that you won't get back, hanging with people who spend money like water, buying things you can't afford, undercharging for your services—these are all areas that cry for boundaries. We'll discuss how to set a budget and track your spending in part two, but for now, think about where you'd ideally like to see your money going, and where it shouldn't be going. That means not going shopping with that friend who's always trying to convince you to buy designer things that aren't even important to you. It also means not going shopping with that cheap friend who makes you feel bad for spending $10 on your favorite lip gloss. No thanks to both!

What Makes an Effective Boundary?

Here's the thing: In order for boundaries to work, you have to actually *enforce* them. Sometimes a boundary can be explicit—you tell the other person exactly what behavior is unacceptable. *I'm not going to loan you any money because you're my friend, and I don't want to take the chance that money could harm our friendship.* If your friend with the guy trouble keeps calling you up with the same old sob story, you can gently tell her, *I'm sorry that happened, but unfortunately, I can't talk about that right now.*

Or a boundary can be implicit. Maybe your boss is used to calling you at all hours of the night. But if you stop answering the phone when she calls late, she'll probably stop calling. If you stop cleaning up after your roommate and just let his dirty dishes sit in the sink—while your clean ones become the only ones left in the cabinet—he's going to get the message that he needs to wash his own stinkin' cups.

Here are some common situations, and the way to set boundaries for them:

Zero Dollar Boundary	Million Dollar Boundary
You regularly check and respond to emails after work hours, even when it takes you away from friends or family, and you never get a break because you never let yourself be off the clock.	You let coworkers know you won't check email after work hours. And you stick with it. You're present when you are with friends and family, and you give yourself a chance to recharge so you're refreshed and energized when the workday starts again.

Even though you know it won't get you anywhere, you talk about your plans and dreams with friends who don't get what you're doing, don't support it, and are never going to see the light.	You have a select group of friends whom you can count on for support and advice. They're ambitious and hustling too, they get what you're doing, and you all want to see each other succeed.
You tell your significant other that if he mistreats you one more time, you're leaving. He does it again, but you stay.	You tell your significant other that if he mistreats you one more time, you're leaving. He does, you end the relationship, end of story.
You take on a freelance job with a set fee for your services. When you turn in the work, your client says he's changed his mind and doesn't want to pay. Instead of enforcing your contract, you grudgingly accept the lost pay and hope for a nice referral.	You take on a freelance job with a set fee for your services. When you turn in the work, your client says he's changed his mind and doesn't want to pay. You firmly remind him of the contract you both signed and insist on being paid for your time and effort.

This all makes sense, right? But I repeat, if you set boundaries and don't enforce them, you're just wasting your time and not making things better for yourself. This can be particularly hard when you're young and don't yet feel comfortable speaking up for yourself, especially if there's a power imbalance.

But if you don't enforce your boundaries, you're sending a message that your boundary doesn't *need* to be respected. When there are no consequences, there's little motivation for the other person to adhere to the boundaries you set. Why should they bother? You're not going to do anything about it. And you know who pays the price when you don't enforce your boundaries? You. You pay in lost time, lost energy, lost wages, lost opportunities. You're moving *away* from your Million Dollar Dream. That's the opposite of a money move.

Reasons You Might Struggle to Set Boundaries

YOU WANT TO BE NICE. As we've discussed, we all want people to like us, but sometimes nice gets in the way of your Million Dollar Dream. You can still be kind, but you may have to let go of being nice. Nice is often performative, done in order to please someone else but at your own personal expense. Also: nice is often a lie where you are pretending you are okay with something you are not okay with. To reach your money goals, you will need to get comfortable with saying no and no longer putting someone else's priorities above your own. My personal rule here is: If I'm doing something nice or generous because it brings me joy, I keep doing it. But if I'm not enjoying it or it feels like a burden, that's a sign I'm locked in for the wrong reasons. Hard pass.

You don't want to disappoint someone. Like being nice, this is often about putting someone else's priorities above your own. Sometimes it feels easier to deal with our own disappointment than deal with the guilt and discomfort of disappointing someone else. But the fact is, life is disappointing. Sometimes people are going to be disappointed. This is true whether or not you've set a boundary. You can't take on the burden of making other people comfortable. No one can be responsible for someone else's feelings. We can each only control our own actions and emotions. It's not your job to be responsible for mine, and it's not my job to be responsible for yours. (Though we may care about others' feelings, we can't possibly control or be responsible for them.) This may not sit well with some people. They might feel offended or even hurt. You're free to try to help them understand why you've set your boundaries if you wish, but you're not responsible for how they ultimately react.

You don't feel like you have the power. Maybe you need to set boundaries with a boss, or a parent, or an elder member of your community. Their age, their status, and their control over some aspect of your life (like a promotion or a monthly check) may make you feel like you can't set boundaries with them. But more often than not, setting boundaries in these situations is more about how you do it. Most people are reasonable and will give you the benefit of the doubt, as long as you explain calmly and firmly why you're setting a certain boundary. So if you explain to your supervisor that you won't be taking on additional responsibilities at work because you take care of your younger siblings when you get home, that will probably make a lot of sense to them. And once you explain it, your grandma will understand that you aren't blowing off that family function she's hosting, you're just out working on your side hustle.

All these reasons amount to a desire to avoid uncomfortable feelings.

A lot of people hold off for that reason. So you're not alone if you find yourself not setting boundaries because of certain circumstances you feel you're in, especially if you're not used to asserting yourself or you haven't felt safe doing so. Always assess the particulars of your situation. First and foremost, make sure you're safe to set a boundary. And if you are, go ahead and set appropriate boundaries to protect your happiness, your integrity, your energy, and your dreams, and be sure to enforce those boundaries as needed.

TRY IT: Go back to the list you made earlier in this chapter. What are some specific boundaries you can set to address these things that are draining you? Make a plan for how you'll enforce them. For added motivation, imagine what you'll be able to do with that extra time, energy, and money you're protecting with your new, healthy boundaries.

Use the Million Dollar Boundaries worksheet for help with this exercise. You can download it at futuremillionaire.me.

This may feel like a lot to commit to (and we haven't even started talking about actual money actions yet!), but millionairing takes effort! Preparing yourself for the journey ahead is critical. Next, we're going to dig into some crucial self-care habits that will make it easier for you to achieve your Million Dollar Dream.

Chapter Summary

- In order to become a millionaire, you will have to set and enforce boundaries.
- Million Dollar Boundaries are a declaration to yourself and others (friends, family, boss, and so on) where you clearly state what you will do, and won't do, in a given situation.

- Million Dollar Boundaries allow you to protect your time, your emotions, and your energy; however, they must be enforced to be effective.
- You might struggle to set boundaries because you want to be nice, you don't want to disappoint someone, or you don't feel like you have the power. Do it anyway.

CHAPTER 5

Self-Care Like a Millionaire

You've done a lot! You have worked on your Million Dollar Thoughts, your Million Dollar Decisions, and your Million Dollar Boundaries. Now it's time to look at some other ways you can prepare yourself to achieve your Million Dollar Dream.

Think about athletes who have their eyes on the Olympics. No one gets to the world's top sports stage without preparation and training, and that's what you've been doing: building mental toughness for your wealth journey. Now we're going to take it to the next level by incorporating your self-care plan into your Million Dollar Dream. Cue the *Rocky* theme.

Remember how I said you're gonna have to work to achieve your dream? Welp, time to work.

The work may look different than you are imagining. Yes, you may have to work to acquire marketable skills that can help you earn more money (like learning sales tactics or photography techniques, for example). You may have to work to build your network or work to build a business. This is what people traditionally think of when they think of work.

The work also includes taking action when you are afraid. It includes smashing limiting beliefs every day, like shutting down thoughts where you are critiquing your body (*I look so ugly*) or your intelligence (*I'm such an idiot!*). It includes asking for the opportunity ("I'd like to be considered for that role")—even when the thought of taking that step makes you want to hurl. And it includes setting appropriate boundaries ("No, I can't hang out tonight") so you are using your time toward your dream.

And there is more work: the work of taking care of yourself. Self-care is what makes all the physical and mental work possible. Think of your wealth-building journey like a marathon not a sprint. You are going to need supportive self-care habits in order to keep running over the long haul. You might think discipline or brute force is what you need here, but that's like running a marathon with no training—difficult, maybe impossible, and definitely unpleasant. When your work toward your Million Dollar Dream is supported by strong care for your mind, body, and soul, it's easier, more probable, and a lot more fun.

So let's talk about the self-care habits that are necessary for you to set yourself up for future success.

Your Body

For starters, take a look at your physical self. Not in that awkward eighth-grade health class way—this is about nurturing your body so that you feel your best. Think about it: How are you gonna make millions if your body is struggling just to get you through the day? You need Million Dollar Energy to make Million Dollar Moves.

Nutrition

Yes, fam, this means being careful about what you put in your body. Eating foods that give you energy is key. Exactly what that looks like will be different for every person. I am not here to sell you on a dietary regimen. What I am saying is to be thoughtful about what you consume and how it impacts your energy, because this too is impacting your bank account.

If you know that eating pizza for lunch makes you feel lethargic and you struggle to get through the rest of the day, but salad with protein actually makes you feel reenergized post-lunch, choose the salad more often than not. If you know that drinking too many sodas and not enough water is going to leave you dehydrated, cranky, headache-y (yep, dehydration does that), and generally uncomfortable and unpleasant, then make it a priority to drink water and take care of your body.

Trust me, I'd rather eat pizza and cake half the time too, but I know it steals my energy rather than giving me energy. So most days I choose not to partake. Don't get me wrong—it's the devil's work that those things taste so good, but we're stronger than that. We care about our bodies more than that. We want to make bank *and* live long enough to enjoy it!

You don't have to start living like a monk. Just like you can't build up wealth overnight, you don't have to make drastic changes immediately and impose deprivation on yourself to improve your energy and physical health. Baby steps. Replace one of your daily snacks with fruit. Add one veggie to your dinner plate. Replace soda with water. And most importantly, pay attention to how different foods make you feel. Then choose the ones that make you feel energized more often.

Sleep

At the risk of sounding like your mother, you also need to get enough sleep. I know there's a mythology that millionaires grind. That they're pulling all-nighters and living off coffee and vending machine snacks. But that's not accurate, it's not sustainable, and it's not necessary. A Real Million Dollar Boss treats their time and body like they treat their money: quite well. As a Future Millionaire, you must value yourself and your time, you must be cautious and measured about how you spend it, and, when you do spend it, you make those expenditures count.

Now, you will have to grind from time to time. For example, when you are building your first side hustle, you are going to work harder and longer to get it off the ground. That's what it looks like to build something out of nothing but your own intelligence, creativity, and skill. However, that is the exception to the rule and not the norm. Even when I was in the early days of my business, I worked a regular job and worked on my business on nights and weekends, but I still got eight hours of sleep. I have never been one to play when it comes to my sleep.

Wearing yourself down is not sustainable. You must keep yourself at peak performance so you're able to do the work necessary to make your Million Dollar Dream come true. Sleep is crucial for lowering your risk for serious health problems, improving your mood, performing better in school and at work, and making good, cognizant decisions, i.e., Million Dollar Decisions.

You will not have good ideas when you are exhausted. Your creativity will suffer if you aren't getting enough sleep. Your professional skills will falter when you're tired. This is one area where you really do not want to follow what your friends are doing, because chances are they aren't getting enough sleep. A 2023 study of sleepiness in young adults showed that 60 percent of folks ages sixteen to twenty-four had moderate to severe sleep deprivation.[1]

MOVEMENT

Nurturing your health also means moving your body daily in ways that feel doable to you. To be clear, this isn't about losing weight. I do not work out to lose weight. I work out because it makes me feel strong, badass, and energized. I strongly believe that all bodies are good bodies. And all bodies deserve to feel good, strong, and energized every day.

We don't realize how much power we have to create energy. If you are feeling really blah and you choose to stretch, take some deep breaths, or do a short burst of exercise (like walking, dancing, or lifting weights), it can change your mood and your energy level in an instant. Yes, boo-boo, you can manufacture energy! Isn't that exciting?

As I hope you are starting to see, Future Millionaires are not victims of their circumstances. Future Millionaires take action to change their circumstances when they're not working for them. And that includes a bad case of the blahs! You literally can shake it to make it.

> **As I hope you are starting to see, Future Millionaires are not victims of their circumstances. Future Millionaires take action to change their circumstances when they're not working for them.**

Time after time, research has shown that movement is linked to happiness. It promotes better mental health. It's good for the brain and helps our thoughts get unstuck. You don't have to become a gym rat (although that's okay too!). Just go do something.

Maybe it's daily walks where you let your mind work out problems while you move, or where you daydream about what your Million Dollar Life will look like, or where you formulate your next big idea. Maybe it's yoga, or swimming, or basketball, or tai chi. Maybe it's putting on some good tunes and dancing like nobody is watching. Or dancing like a whole room is watching. You do you.

If you're not in the habit of exercising regularly, start seeing it as part of your money-making plan. Experiment with different types of movement until you find what works for you, something you enjoy enough to do regularly. Find someone to move with. Turn it into a social outing. Catch up with your friends and dish about each other's money-making journey. That's good for your health too.

MENTAL BREAKS

Taking care of your body also means taking care of your mind. Chasing big goals can wear a person out, and you're getting nowhere fast if you burn yourself out. If you're not already in the habit, start protecting your mental health right now. Like, today! Consider meditation, and prioritize a few minutes of stillness each day. Block it out on your calendar and let your brain just be. It's impossible to maintain the energy you need to make millions if you don't give yourself time and space for stillness.

This also extends to how you spend your spare time. Take breaks from social media and the internet. Disrupt the doom scroll. Find a hobby or activity that will leave you feeling refreshed and recharged.

Maybe you think you'll fall behind if you pause, if you rest, if you take time for a reset. In fact, it's the opposite. Putting yourself and your health first is the biggest money move you can make.

TRY IT: Do a time study! If I say I want to become a millionaire but I am spending all my time playing video games, then my dreams and my actions are not in alignment. Time studies are one of my favorite ways to assess whether I am really focusing my time on what's important to me. Over the course of a week, write down how you are spending your day. What self-care habits are you practicing? What bad habits are sucking up your time or energy? What mental and emotional junk food could you cut from your routine? You may be surprised at what you learn about how you are spending your time, but the beautiful thing is you'll also have the opportunity to do something about it. If you'd like a detailed guide to doing your first time study, download the Million Dollar Time Study worksheet at futuremillionaire.me.

Rest Like a G.O.A.T.

If you ever doubted the importance of rest and recovery, just look at Naomi Osaka and Simone Biles. These women are two of sport's greatest athletes (notice I didn't say *women athletes*; they're great athletes, hard stop), but when they recognized in 2021 that the grind of international competition was compromising their health and safety, they each took a step back.

First it was Naomi, who withdrew from the French Open citing depression and other mental health struggles. Naomi was already a four-time Grand Slam tennis phenom at twenty-three years old, but she recognized that her struggles were affecting not just her performance but, more importantly, her happiness. Despite backlash from many who chose to view her difficult decision as being "entitled," Naomi put herself first, setting a brave example that it's not just okay to take a break, it's crucial. Many others, including OG tennis great Billie Jean King, praised the decision and supported Naomi publicly and privately.

Two months later, Simone Biles withdrew from several events during the Tokyo Olympics. She had developed something known in gymnastics as "the twisties," a potentially dangerous shift in the athlete's perception of her body as it's in motion, which can cause her control to falter. Imagine hurtling through the air in the midst of a twist, intending to perform one motion, but your mind has other ideas. It's an easy way to mis-execute a move and get seriously hurt. As experts later explained, once a gymnast has experienced the sensation once, fear and dread can set in as they worry it'll happen again. Even during one of sport's biggest events, Simone recognized that what she was feeling meant she needed to prioritize her health and safety, and she stepped back from several events, cheering her teammates on instead.

Some people took these decisions as signs of weakness, but in fact Naomi and Simone showed incredible strength by prioritizing themselves.

Their actions also prompted important discussions about the vital need for everyone to protect their mental health, and to seek rest and recovery just as an athlete would with an injury to their physical bodies. Later that same year, other professional athletes—perhaps inspired by Naomi's and Simone's bravery—announced their own mental health struggles and stepped back to prioritize their health, including Atlanta Falcons wide receiver Calvin Ridley and Philadelphia Eagles tackle Lane Johnson.

"Physical health is mental health," Simone Biles wrote on Instagram at the time of her announcement. She couldn't have been more right. So much so, in fact, that she came back to international competition even stronger and more dominant than ever. In the 2024 Olympics, she became the first woman to land the Yurchenko double-pike, won three gold medals and one silver medal, and proved without a doubt that not only is she a legendary athlete of the highest caliber, she's an icon and a role model for putting yourself first.

What these athletes showed to the world and to themselves is that it is not a weakness but an incredible show of strength to make self-care a part of their formula for success. There are times to grind, but there also need to be times to relax, recover, rejuvenate. Being the G.O.A.T. means honoring both.

Your Environment

One of the things about being wealthy I didn't understand when I was young is that you don't have to wait to be rich to start making changes that can make you *feel* rich. It's much easier to maintain an abundance mindset when your environment is reinforcing that abundance to you every day. This isn't about spending money you don't have. It's about treating yourself now the way you want to feel in the future. You're preparing for your future abundance by prepping your environment now.

Begin by doing an audit of your environment. Notice what you are exposing yourself to in your daily physical and digital environment and assess how it makes you feel. You want to notice your physical surroundings, the media messages you are taking in, your home, your wardrobe, your work life, your school life, your daily habits, and your possessions.

Take stock of how each of these things makes you feel. Ask yourself: How is this thing influencing my mood? Is it giving me energy or making me feel drained? If this thing in my environment could talk, what would it be saying to me? If it's saying, "You are gonna be sad and broke forever," drop it, toss it, donate it, or otherwise limit its impact on your daily life. Where you can, replace it with something that makes you feel rich. Even when you are working with a really tight budget, you would be surprised how much power you have to make small changes in your environment that make you feel so much better.

For example, are you eating lunch in a dark, windowless break room or a cafeteria that makes you feel gloomy? Instead, grab your lunch and take it outside to a nearby park to feel some sun on your skin and a light breeze in your hair, and enjoy some shade from a beautiful tree while you eat. It costs you nothing but a little bit of effort to upgrade your daily lunch.

Here's another example: Do you own a bunch of clothing that doesn't fit quite right or doesn't feel like you? Donate those items and head to your nearest trendy thrift store to replace them with fun finds that show off your body and personality. Or do a clothing swap with your best friend to freshen up both of your wardrobes for free.

Maybe you have all your books stacked up on the floor and they regularly fall over and make your space inconvenient and unpleasant. Head to your nearest hardware store, buy some plywood, and borrow a screw gun to make your own bookshelf. You could even get a small can of paint and paint it your favorite color. Your space gets an upgrade, and you'll feel proud that you made your first piece of furniture.

Again, these small upgrades don't have to cost much—or anything. A sprig of something green on your desk or a soft-hued light bulb instead of that harsh overhead florescent one could do wonders for your mood and mindset.

It's not just our physical environments that need an upgrade—our digital environments need one too. What are the first things you see when you open your phone? If you find yourself spending lots of time on Instagram or other social media platforms, following accounts that are always talking about what's wrong in the world, and it brings your energy down and makes you feel defeated, hit unfollow! You will not have the energy to do good work in the world when you are feeling lost.

Likewise, if you follow a bunch of influencers who are living very whitewashed, perfect lives that make you feel bummed out rather than inspired, hit mute and stop watching! Only follow accounts on social media that uplift you, energize you, and inspire you. You do not have to subject yourself to a 24/7 diet of bad news and unrealistic glossy living. If it's not serving you, vanquish it from your life!

This also applies to the books you're reading, the TV shows you're watching, and the podcasts you're listening to. It even applies to friends, family members, and coworkers. Spend time with people, in places and with things that make you feel like anything is possible. You can opt out of the nonstop diet of doom-and-gloom messaging whenever you want. The power is in your hands.

Does this mean that if your friend has a bad day, you should run away from them and never speak to them again? Or that you can never watch a sad movie? Of course not! It just means that you want to ensure you are shifting your environment to receive a lot more positive messages than negative ones.

Once you complete this environmental audit, you will start to notice how much lighter and happier you feel. Not only will you feel better, you'll also sleep better and be that much readier to do the work of becoming a Future Millionaire. When you look around your home and your workspace and feel cared for, and even when you scroll TikTok and see uplifting positive messages that reinforce the notion that you are worthy, it will become easier to make Million Dollar Decisions in every area of your life.

TRY IT: Conduct your own environmental audit. Make a note of what isn't working for you and what could be better. Then brainstorm a list of low- and no-cost ways you can upgrade them and start making it happen. If you want to be guided through this exercise, download the Environmental Audit worksheet at futuremillionaire.me.

Your Language

Can you turn a no into a million dollars? Zandra did! With the right mindset, a no can become the rocket fuel to launch you to incredible things. For then nine-year-old Zandra Cunningham, it led her to becoming recognized by *Entrepreneur Magazine* as one of the youngest self-made millionaires in America. It all started with Zandra's desire for lip gloss. She asked her father for some and he said no. Zandra could have let that be the end of that request. But she asked herself: how can I turn that no into a yes? She did that by deciding to make her own lip gloss using plant-based ingredients.

In her kitchen, Zandra would experiment with different formulations until she came up with a solution she was proud of. With her mother's help, she first sold the products at farmer's markets, then on Etsy. Today, Zandra Beauty offers a range of organic, vegan skincare products that are available across the world in retailers like Target. Now, in addition to being the CEO of Zandra Beauty, Zandra teaches other young entrepreneurs how to start businesses of their own and runs a non-profit to support education for women and girls. All of this success and opportunity came out of Zandra's decision to turn her father's no into a yes for herself and others. Words are important. They can lift you up or crush your spirit. They can inspire you or make you feel defeated. It may sound fluffy, but it's scientifically proven.

According to the research of Dr. Andrew Newberg and Mark Robert Waldman, who wrote the book *Words Can Change Your Brain*, when our mind is focused on uplifting or positive words, there is a positive chemical reaction in our brain. The result of these chemical reactions is that we feel more motivated to take action, our stress and anxiety are reduced, and we feel more relaxed. Over time, focusing on positive thoughts can actually shrink the amygdala, which is the part of the brain that causes us to be afraid, and increase the size of the neocortex, which helps do our most complex thinking. Positive words actually make you bolder and smarter!

So really think through how you talk about yourself and your dreams. Self-deprecating humor may seem funny and lighthearted, but you are literally slowing down your ability to accomplish your dreams when you do. An excellent way to prepare for future wealth is to start working now on the language you use. One of my favorite ways to do this is to start shifting *but* to *and* and start shifting *if* to *when*.

SHIFT FROM BUT TO AND

Think about the difference between *but* and *and*. One closes off alternatives; it's a dead end. The other keeps your options open. It tells your brain, *Hold up, we can figure out a solution.*

This is what Zandra did. She heard no but didn't let it stop her. She might have said, at first, *"I want lip gloss,* ***but*** *my father won't buy it for me."* But after thinking about it and deciding to focus on the opportunity, she changed her tune and said, *"Actually, my father won't buy me lip gloss* ***and*** *I have the ability to make my own lip gloss, so I'm gonna do that!"*

Here's some more examples to consider:

"I want to take my girlfriend out to a nice dinner, ***but*** *I have no money."*

Okay, this is depressing. The word *but* feels like a big stop sign. This Romeo has got no game.

Now how does this version grab you?

"I want to take my girlfriend out to a nice dinner, ***and*** *I have no money."*

See the difference? The word *and* invites you to keep thinking. This isn't a dead end; it's a pesky little hurdle we can find a way around. We just gotta get a little creative.

And what does that creativity look like? Well, there's always the tried-and-true way of saving up your money to make it happen. Nothing wrong with that. But maybe that's too slow, or you're just barely getting by as it is and there's nothing left over to set aside.

What else can you do? You could get a side hustle going to earn more cash for the dinner. (We'll talk more about side hustles in part two.) If you're a good writer, you might pitch an article that requires going to a fancy restaurant and get paid to take your girlfriend out. You might be able to offer your web coding skills to beef up the restaurant's website in exchange for a dinner on the house. Or if you're the musical type and the restaurant has a piano or other entertainment, you could offer your skills in exchange for a gratis meal. The key is not to get stopped by that *but*.

Here's another example:

"I want to ditch the bus and finally buy my own car, ***but*** *I have tons of credit card debt."*

versus

"I want to ditch the bus and finally buy my own car, ***and*** *I have tons of credit card debt."*

Before you count yourself out, research ways to tackle that debt so you can secure a loan and get yourself that car (see chapter 10 for more strategies on managing your money, debt, and improving your credit score). You can look for ways to cut back on your spending and put that money into a fund for a down payment (call it your Hot Wheels Fund). You can monitor Craigslist or other online marketplaces and score a deal on a used vehicle. (But make sure to research the reliability and repair costs for the type of car you're considering, and be careful of scams and offers that might seem to be too good to be true.) There are also tons of resources for managing debt online; I've included some in the appendix.

The point here is that when you think in terms of *and* instead of *but*, you give yourself the space to get creative and find a solution instead of accepting defeat.

Shift from If to When

While I am hanging out with my best friend, Robert, when I say something like, "If I am able to get a book deal . . .", he will immediately stop me and say, "Uh-uh, there is no *if*, there is only *when*. Now try that sentence again." He will literally make me restate what I was saying so that I'm saying *when* rather than *if*. In the moment, this totally annoys me, but Robert is right. The word *when* implies that something is definitely going to happen; the word *if* suggests uncertainty. It suggests that you *hope* that thing is going happen but you don't really *believe* that it will. Don't even entertain those thoughts! As we have already learned, positive language motivates us to take action, which makes it more likely that our Million Dollar Dreams will come true. Let's give it a try.

*"****If*** *I become a millionaire, I am going to donate to causes I care about."*

Sounds positive, right? But it still leaves some room for doubt. Say this instead:

*"****When*** *I become a millionaire, I am going to donate to causes I care about."*

Isn't that so much better? Now you are bursting with excitement at your future life as a millionaire, instead of thinking about the possibility it won't happen.

Whenever you talk about your dreams, declare *when*, not *if*. You are already on your path to becoming a millionaire; that means you are a Future Millionaire right now.

You're reading this book, and you're looking to learn. You're embracing the *and* instead of settling for that *but*. You believe in *when*, not *if*.

Identity Shift

In the bestselling book *Atomic Habits*, author James Clear talks about a subtle mindset shift that speaks to the very way you see yourself. He cites the example of two people who have been smokers and are offered a cigarette. The first person says, "No, thanks, I'm trying to quit." The second person says, "No, thanks, I'm not a smoker."

Technically, both are trying to break the habit of smoking. But the first response leaves room to lapse—the word *trying* opens the possibility that the effort will be unsuccessful. The second response reflects a person who has shifted how they see themselves. They've gone from being a smoker to a nonsmoker. It's a subtle change in phrasing, but it reflects a more absolute—and resolute—shift. The first response speaks to an effort that's still in progress, one from which you can still backslide. The other reflects a complete shift in your identity. You don't see yourself as a smoker anymore. No smokes for you. That simple change eliminates the gray area that might allow you to give in to temptation. If you're a nonsmoker, a cigarette isn't even up for consideration.

Think about how you might apply this insight to your current mindset. Maybe it affects how you dress: pantsuit or sweatpants? *Not today, sweats. I'm a boss and I'm going to look like one.*

Maybe it affects your actions: you know you need to reach out to this person about being your mentor, but you're intimidated and afraid she'll say no. *I'm a Future Millionaire, and Future Millionaires lean into their fears. I'm going to email her right now. If she says no, I know it's not personal and I'll reach out to someone else.*

These kinds of shifts in your language may seem small, but they can pack a real punch. Our minds are so powerful, and we have to arm ourselves with a variety of tricks and tools to make sure our brain is working with us, not against us. Lean into the version of you you're working toward and shift your language to reflect that future identity. In other words, think and talk like you're already the person you want to be.

Making these changes doesn't have to be hard, expensive, or stressful. But doing them will set you up to be your best self—healthy and energized, walking the walk and talking the talk. And, added bonus: they will make you feel like the Future Millionaire you already are.

Chapter Summary

- Future Millionaires take exceptional care of themselves so they have energy for the wealth-building journey.
- Self-care begins with taking care of your body, including eating well, getting enough sleep, moving your body regularly, and taking mental breaks.
- Conduct a time study to understand where your time is going and to help you reclaim your time for self-care and to work toward your Million Dollar Dream.
- Your physical and digital environments impact how you feel and how you show up to your day; conduct an environmental audit and make the changes necessary to make your environment more uplifting.
- Use Million Dollar Language like *and* instead of *but* and *when* instead of *if* to reinforce your belief that the dreams you are working toward are going to happen.
- Making the identity shift from formerly broke person to Future Millionaire will help you to commit to the actions and habits that will help you make this identity a reality.

CHAPTER 6

Friend Like a Millionaire

When I was nineteen, I broke up with my high school boyfriend of five years. I was transferring to a different college and moving away. I had outgrown our drama-filled relationship and wanted the freedom to find myself. I was also becoming an adult and starting to (finally!) fully realize that the way he treated me was not the way I wanted to be treated.

I was interning for then-senator Hillary Rodham Clinton, traveling to Barbados, Ecuador, Nigeria, and France to study and do volunteer work, and otherwise having a very exciting and adventurous college experience. When I returned home to my neighborhood, it was so much fun to spend the summer reconnecting with all my old friends. I also reconnected with my high school boyfriend. We were "just hanging out," I told my friends (they all knew better).

One night we were "just hanging out," and he asked me to join him and a friend for a ride into the city. I can't remember what we were planning to do or where exactly we were going (probably to a restaurant or bar to eat and hang out). All I can remember is crossing the bridge into Manhattan and shortly thereafter hearing sirens go off behind us. We were being pulled over.

And that's when I learned exactly why I'd had an uneasy feeling about this whole evening.

As the driver started to pull over, he revealed he had a gun; an illegal, unlicensed handgun under his seat. Here's what this meant: if the police decided to search the car and found the gun, we would all be going to jail. Never mind it wasn't my gun and I knew nothing about it when I got into the car. This had happened to other people I knew, and the protocol was to arrest everyone in the vehicle.

I was in a trance as I watched the policeman walk over to the car and talk to the driver. All I could see was my future as a lawyer (the dream I had been working toward since I was about eight years old) disappearing before it had even begun. All my hard work in high school and college was about to be wasted due to one bad decision on a warm summer night.

I sat there, frozen, trying to look nonchalant but terrified inside and totally pissed at myself for being in that car and not following my intuition.

The police officer started to ask my ex-boyfriend questions, and then he looked over at me in the back seat and started to ask me questions. I put on the performance of my life, acting like it was no big deal that we'd been pulled over; who knows if it was any good. After what felt like an eternity of Q&A and the cop going back and forth to his police car, and even a little back-and-forth tiff between the cop and my ex as I sat in horror and disbelief ("Why argue with this cop? Have you no plans for the future?!?"), he let us go.

By the time we pulled away, I was a different person. A person who now recognized the value of her own life and dreams.

In those few minutes, I learned that I needed to be a whole lot more selective about the company I keep. I learned that even if I love someone, I could do so from afar and not spend time with them if it was detrimental to my own well-being. I got out of the car a few blocks later and vowed to never, ever get myself into a situation like that again.

The company you keep can literally make or break you. The influence that the people you spend time with have on you is incredibly powerful. That can be a good thing or a bad thing, depending on who you choose to spend your time with.

After that pivotal moment as a young person, I chose to spend my time with positive, loving people who were supportive of my dreams and who were going after their own dreams. I chose people who would inspire me, advise me, cry with me, grow with me, and make me a better person, sister, daughter, friend, and entrepreneur.

TRY IT: Write a list of the top twenty people you spend the most time with and ask yourself, "Are these people helping me grow and be a better me? Or are they preventing me from becoming the person I want to be?" Look at your answers, and consider whether you need to make any changes in terms of who you surround yourself with or how often you spend time with them. Don't be afraid to love someone from afar for the sake of your own life.

Download the Friendship Audit worksheet for further guidance with this exercise at futuremillionaire.me.

You don't have to do any of this alone. You know you've got me here in your corner, but you can and should have a through-thick-and-thin squad of fellow Future Millionaires on your side. This is one of the most powerful secrets to success.

Think of any solo sport or individual endeavor someone has achieved. Think of an actor you admire. A musician, an athlete, an artist. While Beyoncé might be Queen Bey, her achievement would have been impossible without a community helping her behind the scenes. Barack Obama didn't become president of the United States all on his own. Simone Biles, Taylor Swift, LeBron James—all of them are overflowing with talent, dedication, and hard work, but not one of them got to where they are without help and support.

What Should Your Squad Look Like?

Author and entrepreneur John Rohn is famous for observing, "You are the average of the five people you spend the most time with." Science agrees. A study by Harvard social psychologist Dr. David McClelland found that 95 percent of a person's success or failure in life is determined by the people they most regularly spend time with.

It's not that successful people breathe different air than the rest of us. It's that they influence each other in positive ways. They share opportunities.

They learn from each other's expertise and experience. *Avoid this vendor. I used them and they weren't reliable.* Or *Go to this conference; it's really the best one for the type of work you're doing.* If you want success—whether that's in the form of better grades, more money, a thriving business—surround yourself with people who are already doing or working toward those same things.

As my hanging-with-the-wrong-crowd story illustrates, we've all seen this work in reverse. Since we were old enough to know what a *peer* is (and realize that it didn't mean a person who pees, LOL; get it, pe-er . . . never mind), we've been hearing about the dangers of peer pressure. Don't cheat. Don't do drugs. Just say no. But it works the other way too: the habits, work ethic, expertise, and ambitions of our friends rub off on us as well.

Want more evidence? Here you go: A 2015 study conducted by researchers at the HSE Centre for Institutional Studies found that students who hung out with high achievers improved their own performance. And what about those who hung out with underachievers? You guessed it—their grades dropped. The people around you have a big influence on you, so choose wisely.

It's so much harder to reach your full potential when you're hanging out with people who aren't invested in your—and their own—development and success. When you surround yourself with other accomplished people, you all benefit.

Here's some more research that proves it's crucial to build a support system. The American Society of Training and Development did a study about achieving goals—and this is what they found. When you write down a goal privately and you don't mention it to anybody else, you are very *unlikely* to achieve it. However, when you announce your goal to somebody else, like a coach or a friend, you become 65 percent more likely to achieve your goal. And when you schedule a weekly appointment to give a progress report to your coach or friend, you become 95 percent more likely to succeed. Ninety-five percent! I don't know about you, but I like them odds.

Think about attempting a big goal like running a marathon. If you keep this goal to yourself, you *might* get in shape for that race, or you might quit your training plan two months in and no one will be the wiser. And sure, that's fine. No harm, no foul, right? Except that you're no closer to achieving your goal.

But if you tell someone you're training for a marathon, it increases your chances of actually doing so. You're kinda on the hook now. And if you tell someone and ask them to check in on your progress once a week, it increases the likelihood of success even more. Now you're accountable. You do your weekly runs so you can proudly share your results.

Now consider what happens if you convince them to train with you. You're both invested, you're both holding each other accountable, and you've got somebody else going through the challenge alongside you (making the experience a lot more enjoyable). That's the best-case scenario. You're both going to cross that finish line and end up with nice, heavy finishers medals around your necks.

Your squad is everything. For your professional journey, they're your ride or dies, the ones who lift you up and keep you going no matter what. Bottom line: whatever your goal may be—whether it's a health goal, creative goal, or money goal—your odds of achieving this goal go *way up* when you put a support system in place.

Who Should Be in Your Future Millionaire Squad?

Friends and colleagues with similar goals. The people in your inner circle need to be enthusiastic and supportive of your dreams. They should also be ambitious and intentional about achieving their own goals. They should be someone who'll be your wingperson, who'll go with you to events and conferences, who'll review job applications and give you feedback. You both understand that the Future Millionaire status you are pursuing is hard but worthy work, and that it takes vision and intention to reach those goals. You're there to support each other, share resources, comfort each other when you stumble, and generally cheer each other on.

People who support and encourage you. These folks may not share your ambitions, but they are ready and willing to provide support. They respect your hustle and drive and they're here for it. These folks are likely to be your biggest cheerleaders. *Whatever you need, baby, I believe in you and I got you!* If you're trying to slack off, they're the ones who are calling you on it. If you're putting yourself down and doubting that you're ever going to accomplish your goal, they're the ones saying, *Nah, Sis, you know that's not true. I'm not gonna listen to you talk about yourself that way.*

PEERS YOU CAN LEARN FROM. These individuals may not necessarily be friends, per se—you might not confide in them your deepest, darkest fears—but they're people you respect professionally and personally, and you're able to learn from the example they set, as well as turn to them for input and guidance. This is the person you are meeting for coffee to learn more about that side hustle they started.

MENTORS. These are the people who are further along in their journey and can guide you and offer advice through the ups and downs. They have a lot to teach you and are willing to share their biggest mistakes as well as their keys to success. If you don't have access to these folks directly, you may be able to access their knowledge through books, courses, conferences, podcasts, or other content they have created. These folks are invaluable, and we'll talk more later in the chapter about how to find a mentor and nurture that relationship.

TRY IT: What kind of support do you need? Is it emotional support and camaraderie, or professional support and guidance, or some combination of both? What kind of people can give you that support?

Ask yourself the following questions: *I need support with...*

- working through my money mindset.
- figuring out how to make more money and manage it more carefully.
- finding a balance between pursuing my Million Dollar Dream and protecting my mental health.
- ____________ [fill in the blank with what you need].

If you don't know where to look, think about the folks you already know. Is there a coach whose opinions and expertise you trust? Are there people already killing it in the areas you're interested in, people whose paths could help inspire and guide you? Is there a trusted adult in your identity group or faith community? Are there peers who are going through similar challenges who you could trust for support? Don't be shy about seeking resources and support. If you would like help with this exercise, download the Million Dollar Squad worksheet at futuremillionaire.me.

How to Build Your Squad

My best friends are Robert Hartwell (he of the tough love I mentioned above) and Susan Hyatt. Today, we are each other's biggest fans, but it didn't start out that way. It took time and effort to develop friendships like this.

My friendship with Robert started as a business relationship. I began my career as an intellectual property attorney, so I was giving a presentation online about the legal steps you need to take to protect your work from thieves and copycats, and the legal steps to set yourself up for massive revenue growth. Robert was there in attendance, taking notes!

He had recently started his own business, and found out about me from a Facebook ad. He saw a picture of my face on the ad, and he figured, "Okay, here is a successful Black woman talking about business, law, and how to make more money. Sign me up." During the presentation, Robert raised his hand and asked great questions, and that's where we made our first connection.

Shortly after that, Robert invited me to go see an Alvin Ailey dance show. A part of me was like, "This person is literally a complete stranger from the internet." But another part of me said, "It's a fun night on the town!" But I did bring a friend (just in case he turned out to be a scary stalker or something—safety first!). Luckily, he wasn't a stalker. We ended up having an amazing night, and our friendship blossomed from there. Robert is now my very best friend in the world, uncle to my children, and regular Thanksgiving attendee, and it all started with a Facebook ad.

Susan Hyatt is a life coach who hired me back when I was an attorney to handle some trademark work for her. This was early in my career. I really liked her, and we became friendly. I saw the trajectory Susan was on—this little feisty blonde lady was turning her business into a seven-figure empire. She was making serious money. She was hiring employees. She was investing in commercial real estate. And she was doing it while taking fabulous trips to Thailand, South Africa, and Italy.

I was seeing this and thinking, *I'll have what she's having.* So I, in turn, decided to attend one of her life coaching retreats because I wanted to learn, "What are your secrets? How are you living your best life, and what are the moves that I should be making?"

Gradually, over the course of several years, our relationship deepened into a really close friendship. We went to hang out at her lake house together. We'd meet up in New York City for a bougie brunch. And we supported each other through so many ups and downs.

Robert, Susan, and I live in different areas of the country, so we have to make an effort to keep our relationship strong. This means checking in via text every day. And planning trips in advance. We'll get together four to five times a year and do a weekend trip or retreat. Even though we don't see each other in-person every single week, we stay connected daily via our group chat. Then during those trips, we pour tons of energy into our friendship and refill the cup.

Let me tell you, these two friends have literally added *millions* of dollars to my life. They help me brainstorm money-making ideas, they give excellent advice, and we have collaborated on business projects. And they've added emotional riches to my life—hours of laughter, incredible memories on vacations, and the knowledge that no matter what happens, these two people have my back. That's priceless.

What's the lesson here?

Number one: When you find someone who is doing what you want to be doing, you need to go spend time with that person. Let's say you see someone who is running a successful business, or investing in the stock market, or getting tons of scholarships, and you're like, "I want that life!" When you see that person who's living your dream life, go learn from them!

Make an effort to meet them. Exchange numbers. Send a text and follow up. Bring this person into your life. Gradually, a real friendship might develop. You need to go learn from this person because they have something important to teach you. And you can be a light in their life as well.

Friendship lesson number two: You have to make an effort. Take the initiative. Invite someone to see a movie. Plan a fun gathering. Get your butt in the car and go to their birthday party. Or start a group chat and share hilarious memes in there, on the regs. Friendships do not bloom unless you water them.

Hopefully you have some affirming people in your squad already, but it's always good to meet new people who share your areas of interest. How do you find those people?

LOOK AROUND YOUR NEIGHBORHOOD, CLASSES, OR WORKPLACE. You might have a neighbor, classmate, or colleague who's as motivated as you. Consider inviting them out for coffee and have a casual chat about your respective goals. You might find that you have a lot more in common than you realized.

BECOME A JOINER. This can be challenging if you tend to be more reserved, but it's soooooo worth it. If talking to people you don't know sounds like your personal nightmare, you might need to find more intimate events that feel less intimidating to start or bring an extroverted wingperson to support you.

Pick an event or gathering that matches your interests and challenge yourself to strike up a conversation with at least one person there. Introduce yourself and ask them questions about themselves. The easiest way to initiate a conversation is to let other people do the talking first.

You can also look for someone who seems as uncomfortable as you feel. Maybe they're standing over by the bean dip and trying not to look at their phone. Think of how relieved they're going to be when you saunter over and say hi. You also don't have to stick with just professional gatherings. There are clubs for runners and bikers. Clubs for hikers, chess players, Roblox enthusiasts, movie lovers—you name it. And since these groups are built around an activity, that can make the conversation part much easier.

Who's lagging at the back of the pack (or cruising up front) who you can chat up for camaraderie? Who's struggling to fix their flat, who you can help and make a new friend?

Ideally, you'll want some folks in your squad who share your beliefs and your ambitions, but resist the temptation to make these relationships transactional. There's no room for a *What can you do for me?* mentality here. You're looking for your squad, sure, but the best squads are built on true affection, connection, and respect for each other. In other words, be real and reciprocate. Don't try to force a friendship with a person who is not your cup of tea.

Reconnect with the community you already have. As the saying goes, "To get a friend, be a friend." Reconnect with folks you may have lost touch with. Send them a card reminiscing about something the two of you shared. Set up a regular time to walk with someone you haven't seen in a while. Become active in a group that was meaningful to you but that dropped off your radar. These renewed relationships don't have to be directly connected to a professional interest. Sometimes it's important just to have people in your life who knew you from an earlier time, and when you reconnect and support each other in the present day, that earlier bond is strengthened even more.

Create your own community. If you haven't quite found your people, or you don't know anyone else in your network who likes to do a certain thing that you enjoy, start your own group. Maybe you like soccer. Or watching the films of Akira Kurosawa. Wouldn't it be great to find others who love hip-hop as much as you do? Or who share your passion for social justice? This group can be virtual or IRL. Share news of the group with friends and colleagues. (Who knew Naomi from Statistics liked anime too?) Post it on social media. Ask early members to invite others who might be a good fit, to keep growing the group.

Choose Your Million Dollar Squad

Which seven people would make up your Million Dollar Squad? They can be living or not. (Mine would include Beyoncé, Oprah, Viola Davis, Madam C. J. Walker, and Serena Williams.) What characteristics do you admire about these people? When you're making important life decisions, these are voices you can turn to. For me, I know that Beyoncé and Serena would tell me I'm going to have to work hard for what I want, because that's what they do. Oprah would say to live your best life, you have to live your truth. Madam C. J. Walker believed in herself despite her circumstances. If she could make herself a millionaire during the times in which she lived, Lord knows we can overcome the obstacles we might face. Viola would remind me to believe in my own excellence, deliver that, and then trust that it is enough. All these women are trailblazers that I admire and that I want to emulate.

Your Million Dollar Squad is likely to be people you admire because something about what they're doing is also true for you. If you spot it, you got it! You have the talent to do something similar. What traits do you admire in your Million Dollar Squad? Maybe include a quote from them. How do they handle controversy? How do they handle difficulty? How would the people in your Million Dollar Squad advise you? Read their books, and if they're doing a talk, go see them speak. Learn as much as you can about them so that they help "guide" you on your million-dollar journey.

TRY IT: Write a description of your ideal real-life squad. What kinds of people are you looking for? What do you hope to do together? This can help you articulate exactly what you want from this ideal group. You don't have to share it with anyone, although you can! Download the Million Dollar Squad worksheet for more guidance at futuremillionaire.me.

How to Find a Mentor

If we all agree that it takes a village to raise a millionaire (and we do!), then we agree that every village needs its wise elders. A mentor is the true heart of any professional squad. This is often somebody within your chosen profession who is further along in their career and can offer guidance and wisdom as you travel your own path. Sounds great, right?! So how do you find this magical person? And what are the rules of engagement?

First, you should spend some time thinking about what you're looking for in a mentor. Do you just want someone you can bounce questions off, or turn to for guidance when you're navigating something tricky at work? Or are you looking for someone who will meet with you regularly, listen to your goals and obstacles, and help you get there? Be mindful, too, that this is a two-way street. Think about what you can offer them in return.

What are your goals for your mentor relationship? Do you envision it as a short-term one (say, just a few months)? Or do you hope for something longer-term? Do you envision meeting regularly or periodically? Before you ever pick up the phone or shoot off an email, be sure about what you are asking of them.

Many leaders see mentorship as an important way to give back or to help pull someone else up. Many people enjoy the process of teaching what they've learned during their own careers. Seeing a young person they've helped succeed can be very satisfying. But a mentor will also want to know that you'll respect their experience and expertise. This doesn't mean you have to do everything they say, but you want them to know that you're willing to listen to their guidance and you're open to implementing their advice.

Mentors will want to know that you're serious about the mentorship relationship; they don't want to waste their time. If they feel good about your goals and vision, they may recommend you for positions or other networking opportunities down the road, and they want to know that you'll live up to their recommendation. No one wants to recommend someone only to have that person fall short, which could reflect poorly on the mentor. So be prepared, show up—on time!—for all scheduled mentorship meetings, do the work (if they suggest any), and represent yourself and your mentor well.

But Rachel, where do I find these mythical mentors? This is where you lean into that network you've started building. Who do you admire at work or within your goal profession? Who do your friends know, or your parents' friends? Are there people you admire from previous jobs, from your spiritual groups, or from community organizations?

Social media can also be helpful. Who do you follow on Instagram or LinkedIn who speaks knowledgeably about the professional areas you're interested in? What podcasters speak to the topics you want to explore?

Who has the career you wish for yourself? Who has traveled a path similar to yours, who might be able to offer guidance about how to navigate the kinds of challenges you might face?

Once you've identified some strong mentor candidates, it's time to make the ask. First, be prepared. Know your elevator pitch—the summary of what you're looking to discuss, given in a few sentences. Know what kind of time commitment you're asking of them, and how frequently you're hoping to meet. Be prepared to be flexible. They may have much less time than you envision, but if they're someone you truly admire and believe you can learn from, any time with them is likely to yield valuable insights.

Let them know what has drawn you to their work. What is it about them or their accomplishments that makes you want to learn from them? Also be prepared with some suggestions about what you can offer to them in exchange for their mentorship. Maybe you could provide some personal assistant work once a week. Maybe they could use some social media expertise from a young person more tuned-in to TikTok than they are. Maybe they'd just appreciate a baked good every now and then. Consider what kind of extra help they might need, and be sure to include how you can help with that in your pitch.

Try to make it as easy for them as possible. If their schedule is tight and they seem reluctant to meet face-to-face, suggest a twenty-minute informational interview over the phone or via Zoom. When you go into that meeting, be prepared with specific talking points that align with your goals for the experience. Be prepared to follow their lead if the conversation veers from what you've envisioned, but also know that it's okay to gently redirect things with questions from your talking points if the conversation goes off course.

During the call, be open to feedback and critique. It's okay to ask follow-up questions to help you better understand their feedback, but resist the temptation to get defensive. Take notes during your meetings, so you have a record of the mentorship and can refer back to their guidance at a later date.

Remember boundaries. Respect your mentor's time, and their own boundaries. (A mentorship isn't free therapy or a chance to just complain!)

And, as with any situation where there's a power imbalance, protect your own boundaries as well.

Whether your squad is some of your fellow Future Millionaires all hustling together, or a mixture of peers and experts you've gathered to meet a range of needs on your professional journey, your squad is invaluable. Not only do they provide insights, support, expertise, and camaraderie, but they will make this journey so much less lonely, and so much more fun. My friends make my life better, they help me to live in abundance, and thanks to them, I'm emotionally, mentally, and, sure, materially richer every single day.

Chapter Summary

- The people you spend time with can have a profound impact on your life. Future Millionaires have a Million Dollar Squad made up of people who are positive, ambitious, supportive of their dreams, and have something to teach them.
- Conduct a friend audit and determine if the people you are currently spending most of your time with are the kinds of people who will propel you forward or drag you down.
- Research shows that 95 percent of a person's success or failure in life is determined by the people they most regularly spend time with. Choose wisely.
- If you want to build a Million Dollar Squad, you are going to have to make an effort—to gain a friend, be a friend.
- Create a list of the people you want to be on your Million Dollar Squad and then put in the work to connect with those people, one way or another.
- Find yourself a mentor within your chosen profession who is further along in their career and can provide guidance and wisdom toward your Million Dollar Dream.

You Have Finished Part One

Take a moment to pause. Celebrate all the work you've completed so far.

I want to stop and take a moment to say: good job! You've done a lot of the hard work already. So give yourself a pat on the back, put on your favorite song, and do a little celebratory dance for investing in yourself and committing to the process!

Now that we've discussed how to prepare to be a Future Millionaire, it's time to talk money moves. You've successfully graduated to part two!

PART TWO

Get Money

CHAPTER 7

Value Like a Millionaire

Okay, friends, time to really get into it. You've determined your Million Dollar Dream. You've learned about thought work—you understand the importance of reframing negative thoughts and rewording the stories that cause harm. You've prepared for the work ahead: You're making mindset shifts, ditching those Zero Dollar Decisions, and setting boundaries like a true Future Millionaire. You're taking care of your body by eating healthfully, getting rest, and carving out space to reset. You've adopted new language to use and are building up your very own Million Dollar Squad.

Now that you've got your mind right, it's time to get your pockets right. Yes, it's time to . . . GET. THIS. MONEY.

And getting this money begins with learning to value yourself like a millionaire. That means taking stock of your passions, skills, experiences, interests, ideas, and talents to determine the value you have to offer this world . . . in exchange for a million dollars, of course.

As we begin this second half of the book, I want to be very clear: When I say we are going for a million dollars, I mean we are going for a million dollars. Your Million Dollar Dream is not hypothetical. It is very real and it is very possible. It's also very doable.

As we start to get into the work of making a million dollars happen in your life, you may have feelings of fear creep in. You may think, *Who do I think I am?* Maybe a friend will tell you to "be realistic." Maybe you'll convince yourself that you are just setting yourself up for disappointment. These thoughts are normal. In fact, they are a part of the process. Every current millionaire was once a Future Millionaire filled with fear. They had to face these thoughts, reframe them, and choose to believe in the future they desired. They had to take action despite their fears. And one day they proved themselves right. You will too as long as you don't give in to the fear or give up on your Million Dollar Dream. One foot in front of the other, one step at a time, you will make this dream happen. And I will be cheering you on as you do.

These are the exact steps that helped me go from zero money, zero network, and zero resources to becoming a millionaire. If I could do it, then you can do it too.

But don't take my word for it, take Sadie's. Sadie is a client of mine who has successfully become a millionaire at a very young age.

Sadie's Story

Sadie had a crush. Little did she know that this crush, at only twenty-two years old, would lead her down an incredible path to entrepreneurship.

You see, Sadie's crush was allergic to gluten. So she decided to experiment with some recipes and make him some delicious gluten-free bread. Many of those attempted bread loaves went into the trash, but when one came out really well, Sadie asked her crush to give it a try. It turns out he loved it!

After discovering she was gluten-intolerant as well, she doubled her efforts to make the most delicious gluten-free sourdough bread. (She was really into baking bread!) At the time, she only had $100 in the bank. Her crush-turned-boyfriend helped kickstart her venture by buying $300 worth of ingredients in exchange for $300 of bread credit to use later (she charged him full price for the bread too!).

"I emailed everyone I knew in the Bay Area (about forty people) and told them I was starting my company and that they could pick up bread from my apartment," says Sadie. "I sold thirteen loaves of bread the first week. One of my friends shared the email, and a friend of a friend ordered three loaves. She turned out to be the catalyst—she worked in an allergy clinic and started to tell all her clients who needed to eat gluten-free food about my bread. One of those clients told her parents' group, and one of those parents was a reporter who wrote an article about me. The business went full time six weeks after the article came out."

Once she had a clear proof of concept, her dad pitched in $3,000, which helped Sadie propel her business forward. Nine months later, it was undeniable—Sadie's new business, Bread SRSLY, was a hit.

Sadie recalls having to be resourceful as she worked to get the business off the ground. Because she didn't drive, initially she had to rely on friends for deliveries. When one friend who had promised to drive her around to help make deliveries stood her up at the last minute (he was out surfing!), Sadie had to resort to delivering bread herself by bicycle. Her unconventional delivery method inadvertently sparked local interest and helped to raise awareness of the business.

"When I started getting local press, the articles really focused on the bike delivery aspect! Even though we don't do that anymore, I am convinced that the biking was actually what got the word out."

In its first full year, Bread SRSLY earned $33,000. Today, the business makes $2.1 million per year!

Sadie now has a full-time team to manage the day-to-day tasks (like deliveries!) so she can work on the high-level strategies for the business. One of the things she is working on is developing a wholesale strategy to get her bread into local supermarkets around the country.

What began as a project to woo her crush turned into an amazing career where Sadie gets to earn great money, help people with gluten allergies, and provide her full-time team with an amazing place to work. And yes, Sadie also managed to snag her crush, who is now her husband.

As you can see from Sadie's story, opportunities to make money can come from anywhere. Thanks to her crush, Sadie realized she had a passion for developing recipes and helping people with gluten allergies. There are so many ways to increase your income; all you have to do is choose the right one for you. The key is to make it not just about the money. You'll enjoy your work more if it gives you a sense of purpose.

What Are You Passionate About?

Maybe you already know what career you want to pursue. Maybe you're already doing the thing—purchased the books, chosen the major, bought the T-shirt. If so, bravo! If not, no worries. I got you. There are so many voices out there shouting about what you could be doing for your j-o-b. Maybe you're hearing "AI" this or "start-up" that. But the key to a million-dollar career isn't following what's hot right now. It's leaning into your natural passion and talents. Longevity and persistence in your career come from making a commitment, and that commitment comes from doing something you enjoy and you feel passionate about. So stop right now and ask yourself, ***What do I really love, and what do I do that can be valuable?***

Maybe you already know what you're good at. Or maybe you have no idea. As a young person, it's easy to think you don't yet have skills or talents that someone would shell out money for. But you know what? You're wrong! Maybe you're still finishing school. Or maybe you're already working to help support your family. Or maybe college wasn't for you and you're out there hustling the best you know how. If you're reading this book, if you've gotten this far, if you've taken the initiative to dream your Million Dollar Dream, you've got what it takes to turn your skills and passion into money.

So let's break this down into some small, easy steps:

1. Think About What You Are Naturally Good At

How do you spend your free time? Are you good at fixing computers? Are you a gaming guru? Are you a whiz at styling people's hair? Do you know your way around a toolbox? Do you know how to really work a turntable? Maybe you are an excellent writer or are good at presenting in front of an audience. Maybe you're a fashionista and it's a no-brainer to style fly outfits. Or you can whip up a fancy pizza or an amazing chocolate pie like nobody's business. Whatever it is, it's something you do because it feels good, and it probably puts you in your happy place.

Think about the things you do for funsies, things that don't feel like work. You're using skills for these activities just like you do with anything else, but because they don't feel like work, you may dismiss them as a path to a potential job. For example, do you love planning group trips or fabulous slumber parties for your friends? Maybe there is a career in travel planning or project management in your future. We spend our free time doing the things we enjoy most, so why not let your passion guide you to your profession?

Start by making a list of the things that come naturally to you. In school, there were probably subjects you loved because they weren't a struggle, you were good at them, and they sparked your interest and got you excited. Those subjects are a good place to start. Is it science? Is it PE? Is it art? Is it reading and writing? There are no wrong answers here.

For me, it was being a talker. Whenever report cards would come home, mine would always compliment me for my good grades, and then snitch to my mama that I needed to talk less! What can I say? I had a lot to share, and I shared it loud and proud! But look at me now, right?! Your girl makes the big bucks for being a nonstop talker. One of my favorite parts of what I do is getting up on stage and talking to audiences about how they can grow their own skills to become a success.

I'm not the only one who gets paid to run their mouth! Think of the comedians you love. I guarantee you they were class clowns as kids. They probably drove their teachers and families crazy, always goofing off and trying to get a laugh. Well, look at them now.

TRY IT: Take a few minutes right now to write down three things you can do naturally and easily. Think about the things people compliment you for. Do you get praised for how naturally neat you are? Bingo! You might be the future CEO of a home organizing empire, the next Marie Kondo. Maybe your friends constantly thank you for being their biggest cheerleader. Voila! Maybe you've got what it takes to run a thriving fitness studio or life coaching practice. Don't be swayed by thinking *Nobody will ever pay me to do XYZ.* Actually, people will pay you (and pay very well), because what comes naturally to you does not come naturally to others. Since they can't do it, your skills seem alluring, even mysterious and magical. So go on, work your magic! They. Will. Pay. You. For. It

If you would like help with this exercise, download the Million Dollar Value worksheet at futuremillionaire.me.

(Note: keep this completed exercise handy, as you'll need the list again in chapter 9.)

2. Make a List of Your Accomplishments

Look at your past and make a list of the things you've done that make you valuable. Did you get Perfect Attendance at school? It may seem trivial, but it's not! You're reliable. That's *hugely* valuable. Add that to your list, Future Millionaire.

You made straight As? They don't hand those out to just anybody. You're a hard worker who knows how to study and doesn't give up? Add that to your list. Are you patient with the customers at your burger shack job? Write that down: You're good at customer service. Do you take on tasks when you see something at your job that needs to be done? Yeah, you do! That means you take initiative. And pride in your work.

Million Dollar Value: *(noun)* The innate skill, ability, experience, and/or talent that you possess that also has the potential to make you millions of dollars.

What else? Did you have the favorite cupcake at the church bake sale, which sold out before everybody else's? Did you get your best friend elected class president because you have a keen instinct for strategy? Are you an ace at hoops and helped lead your teammates to the regional finals? Did Mrs. Knox start pulling you from class every time her computer froze, because she knew she could count on you to fix it? Are you the one who always coaxes your friends to hit the weight room, then helps them get through their reps when you're there?

Take my niece, for example. She learned how to do makeup from her mom, who was really talented and did elaborate things with makeup. When my niece was in college, her friends saw what she could do and started hiring her to do their makeup for school events, parties, and class pictures. She started out with a side business, just doing makeup for her friends and advertising makeup products as a social media influencer, then turned those accomplishments into a full-blown career when she got a job with the makeup company MAC. Now she gets paid to be a full-time makeup artist in her day job *and* still has her side hustle doing makeup for weddings, photo shoots, and other special events. Dollar-dollar bills, y'all!

TRY IT: Take another look at your list and add any big accomplishments or milestones you've achieved. Do you notice any patterns emerging? Your list is proof: You *do* have valuable skills. You're probably using them regularly. And you can put them to work to make you stacks.

More guidance for this exercise is provided in the Million Dollar Value Worksheet, which you can download at futuremillionaire.me.

3. Take an Assessment

Another super useful tool is a skills and personality assessment, which can help you learn more about the kinds of things you're naturally talented at. I often ask my clients and employees to take the CliftonStrengths assessment. It's one of my favorites, although I also like Kolbe and DISC. Each works in a slightly different way, but they all ask you to answer a series of questions about your personality, skills, and talents. Based on your answers, the results can provide clues and insights into the kinds of professions that might suit you best.

You can find skills assessments online, although some cost a small amount of money. CliftonStrengths isn't free (it's under $50), but they offer student discounts. You can take DISC for free on certain websites. Check the appendix at the end of the book for links to all of these. Even if there is a cost, this may be one of those situations I talked about in part one, where you should see one of these tests as an investment in yourself. If you're not sure what you're interested in or the kinds of careers you might be good at, or even if you do, it's worth it to get to know yourself better and to understand what opportunities are out there for someone with your personality type and natural talents.

How Do You Like to Work?

In addition to *what* you want to do, I also want to encourage you to think about *how* you prefer to work. Not just what you're doing on a day-to-day basis, but how you're doing your job. Think about what the mechanics of the jobs you are considering really are. If you're an introvert, you may like studying the topic of finance, but you may hate the chaos and high pressure of the trading floor. Other areas of finance would probably be a better fit for how you show up for work; maybe you would love spending your day organizing data and running complex calculations on a spreadsheet all alone with no one bothering you. Or you may be a super extroverted journalist, and you may like the times when you're out interviewing people but hate the times when you're closed up in your home office, pounding away at your keyboard and feeling like a shut-in.

For me, I was a kid who was fascinated by courtroom dramas on TV, and that's how I decided I was going to be a lawyer. I am more extroverted, so I imagined myself standing before a judge and a jury, arguing passionately for the rights of my clients. Fast-forward to me, fresh out of law school. I'm working for a corporate firm and sitting in front of my computer most of the day. I spent *a lot* of time drafting contracts by myself. So many contracts! (And if you've ever read a contract, you know that those things are DRY. Not much room for my vigor and good intentions amid all those *herewiths* and *whomsoevers*.)

There were very few occasions where I was actually able to argue for my client in court, and even interaction with my clients was pretty limited. Most of my time was spent doing legal research and drafting legal documents. It felt like a bait and switch. I didn't sign up just to do paperwork!

What I imagined the work of a lawyer to be was very different than what the practice of law actually was for me.

Now, as a business coach, I give speeches all the time. I am working with groups of entrepreneurs every week. I'm recording podcasts and making videos for social media. With my shift to coaching, I changed *how* I show up to work. Now I really am able to get up in front of audiences and help people. Just like Little Rachel imagined!

If you're not exactly sure how you like to work best, another tool you could use is the Myers-Briggs Assessment. This one asks you a series of questions to determine what your personality type is and where you fall on a spectrum between extrovert and introvert, intuitive and observant, thinking and feeling, judging and perceiving. Based on your answers, the results will suggest careers that pair well with those particular qualities.

So an INFJ, for example, is someone whose personality identifies them as more on the Introverted, Intuitive, Feeling, and Judging end of the spectrum. Our culture tends to lift up extroverts, but you introverts are often the ones actually holding everything together. We need y'all! INFJs are compassionate and empathetic, driven by a deep sense of purpose. Does this sound familiar? If so, you might find yourself leaning toward professions that fulfill that need: INFJs often become teachers, therapists, spiritual leaders, or nurses. INFJs also tend to be strong communicators and creative types, including writers, video game creators, photographers, musicians, or other creative professionals.

INFJs may prefer a quiet workplace, and because they already have a strong sense of fairness and morality, they don't need some scoldy supervisor wagging a finger at them. They're guided by their work ethic, and they do well just being left alone to get the dang thing done already, *thankyouverymuch*.

These kinds of tests aren't the end-all, be-all, but they can be really helpful for understanding your particular personality traits, so you have a better sense of both the type of work that suits you best as well as the work environment where you're most likely to thrive.

Think of all this internal work as a way to study your greatest asset on the path to making millions: you! The more you know yourself, the easier it is going to be to uncover *your* right path to millions.

How Do You Decide?

With all this information gathering and listening to your inner work nerd, you may be wondering, *What do I do with all this? How do I decide on the right career?*

First of all, keep in mind that it's not realistic to love your job 100 percent of the time. There are almost always going to be aspects that you don't enjoy. So don't run from job to job thinking you have to find the one thing that you love doing *all* the time. Instead, aim for a career that you enjoy at least 70 percent of the time. Also, aim to do something where you learn a marketable skill. Keep this in mind even as you're choosing classes in school. Follow your interests and curiosity, but also try to make sure you study something that gives you a marketable skill, i.e., a skill you can sell.

If you learn to write marketing copy, if you learn how to do research, if you learn how to read and draft architecture plans, or take great photos, or edit videos, these are all skills that you can tout to potential employers and take with you into future jobs. As a bonus, you can parlay these skills—whether you learn them in school or on the job—into something you can sell later in your work as an entrepreneur. I was able to use my legal expertise and communication skills to open my own firm. If you learn sales or how to write papers, or how to create PowerPoint presentations that are really impactful, you can put these skills to work for you long after you finish school or leave that job.

So how do you decide? Here are five parameters that can help you make a Million Dollar Decision about the next step on your path to your Million Dollar Career:

1. **INTEREST.** This is critical. If you aren't excited by it, then it probably doesn't interest you. It's really hard to get good at things you have no interest in. Don't rely on discipline alone. Follow your curiosity. If a particular career path sounds like something you'd love to dive into, know more about, and gain experience in, you are on the right path.
2. **MONEY.** As we have already established in this book, money matters. You want to be paid well, of course, because why are we all

gathered here if not to learn how to gain financial freedom? Harvard professor Arthur C. Brooks teaches about and writes extensively on happiness. In a recent article in *The Atlantic* magazine, he writes that while money alone can't buy happiness, "having the money to pay for experiences with loved ones, to free up time to spend on meaningful activities, and to support good causes does enhance happiness."[1]

3. **Joy.** Being happy at work is not something to be underestimated. Just think about it: Most people spend eight hours per day at their job for a total of forty hours per week. That's a third of your life, so you better enjoy it; otherwise, it will have a profoundly negative impact on the quality of your life overall. You'll be happiest in a job that brings you joy *and* meaning.
4. **Meaning.** Brooks suggests two things that make work meaningful for most people: *earned success* (which he describes as "a sense of accomplishing something valuable") and *service to others.*[2] Having a sense of purpose in our work is an invaluable part of happiness. Don't overlook that in the effort to make more money.
5. **Values.** Make sure your work aligns with your values. Don't take a job just because of the money, especially if the work itself turns your stomach or makes you feel uncomfortable for any reason. I found myself in exactly this position when I was offered a job at a law firm that represented companies in the oil and gas industries. I *needed* that job. The salary was over $100,000, and I had more than $300,000 of student debt. But I couldn't bring myself to say yes. I knew I'd be defending companies that were overtly doing harm to the environment, and worse, denying their responsibility for that harm. I spent so much time thinking and worrying about whether to take the job that the firm eventually rescinded the offer. And let me tell you, they did me a favor! So trust your gut. If something about the job feels wrong to you, it's probably wrong *for* you. More than anything, you have to feel good about the work you do and the company you do it for.

You may not find a job that checks all five boxes right out of the gate, but as you keep working toward the career that's best for you, eventually you will. As Brooks advises, "Do not fall prey to seeking pure happiness. Instead, seek lifelong progress toward *happierness*."[3] Education, career, financial freedom, joy—they're not a destination, they're a journey, and one that lasts throughout your life. When you learn to embrace that journey, to seek happ*ier*ness, that's when you know you're on the right path.

TRY IT: Now that you've seen your skills and interests for the moneymakers they are, let's see what you can do with that information. Spend some time thinking about how you'd like to work, as well as the skills and personality traits you might have discovered if you took a skills assessment or the Myers-Briggs. (No worries if you haven't been able to tackle those yet, though!) Now list ten careers you might be interested in. Don't worry if you don't have all the certifications or degrees you might need. Nobody's going to ask you to perform brain surgery tomorrow! Just start zeroing in on the types of work you think might suit you best. And pay particular attention to anything you find yourself getting excited about. That's a very good sign that you're heading in the right direction!

For more guidance in completing the Try It exercises in this chapter, download the Million Dollar Dream worksheet at futuremillionaire.me.

What If I Get It Wrong?

One thing that people don't talk about enough when it comes to careers is this: You probably won't get it right the first time. I mean, think about it. The chances of you knowing exactly what you want to do for the rest of your life . . . right now?? That's very rare. *And that's okay!* There are no wrong turns. There are no mistakes. Every job you take, every passion you pursue, every curiosity you follow, you're learning skills that you can apply to the next thing you do.

Even if you hate what you're currently doing, you're gaining experience and insights you can use down the road. Maybe it's how to work with a certain software program that will come in handy later. Maybe it's how to be patient with a challenging boss, or firm with a difficult coworker. Maybe it's just getting practice at being resilient in the face of difficult circumstances. Every avenue you pursue, you're learning what you like and what you don't like for your career. You're learning how you want to engage with people, and you're learning from others' behavior how *not* to behave. All experiences are valuable, even if the value is just in the relief and perspective you get once you're seeing them in the rearview mirror on your way out!

Plenty of people don't figure out what they *really* want to do until they've tried several other careers first. It's not at all uncommon to be well into your thirties before you finally find the thing that suits your passions and talents the best. All that is to say, follow your instincts and don't get too hung up on trying to get it "right" straight out of the gate. (What even is "right"??) Do *something*. Yes, *anything*! Get experience. Acquire skills. Follow your inklings. If something piques your interest, follow it.

And don't sweat it if you feel like the clock is ticking and you haven't found *it* yet. Every experience teaches you something you can take into whatever comes next. When I was sweating it out at that law firm, I was definitely not in my Feel-Good Era. But the skills I learned in law school and in that job have continued to serve me well. I'd even say I wouldn't be as successful today without those experiences. I honed my public speaking skills in the mock trials we did in law school. In the seven years I practiced law, I learned to write well, because we were taught to cross out every word we didn't need, to go line by line through our work, to be brief but clear. So even though I ultimately realized that growing businesses is my passion, those seven years weren't a waste. Nothing you learn is wasted. A false start is not a dead end.

Now that you understand the value you bring to the marketplace and have some idea of the work you might like to do, let's discuss how to make that next great career move.

Chapter Summary

- In order to become a millionaire, you have to value yourself like a millionaire. That means taking stock of your passions, skills, experiences, interests, ideas, and talents to determine the value you have to offer this world . . . in exchange for a million dollars, of course.
- The key to a Million Dollar Career isn't following what's hot right now. Instead focus on your Million Dollar Asset (you!) by considering your natural skills and talents, making a list of your past accomplishments, and taking personality assessments. The right way to add value to the world is the way that is a good fit for who you are.
- Seek career opportunities that align with your interests, make money, allow you to have joy at work, give you meaning, and align with your values.
- The thing that will make you a millionaire may not be the first thing you try. Instead, follow your instincts and take the next step.

CHAPTER 8

Work Like a Millionaire

In the summer of 2010, Lindsey Zahn had just finished her first year of law school. She had two more years to go before she graduated, but she did not waste any time getting ahead when it came to her post-graduate job search. She did something I had never seen before, and I thought it was one of the smartest moves a student could make. It was one of those things that I wished I had thought of myself.

Lindsey had studied hospitality in college and was planning to become a lawyer. She did not know exactly how she would marry those two degrees together, but she hoped she would come up with a plan before she graduated. Unlike Lindsey, many of her college classmates were very clear on exactly what they wanted to do upon graduation. She was jealous of their certainty. Lindsey had just pursued her interests. She was interested in hospitality, so she studied it in college. Then she was interested in law, so she decided to apply to law school. No real plan other than she hoped all this education would eventually lead to a career she would love.

Her final semester of college, she took a Restaurant Management class, where her professor assigned an article about a fancy Italian wine that several wineries had been fraudulently producing. A whole legal case took place because of the wine laws these wineries had broken. Before then, Lindsey didn't even know wine law existed. Her interest was piqued. She got excited.

Then she remembered a piece of advice her father had given her: "The riches are in the niches." Okay, okay, Lindsey's father didn't say *that exactly.*

But he did teach her the importance of differentiating herself from her competitors. Lindsey's father was a businessman, and he taught her to identify niche markets and then become an expert in that niche; this was how she could provide Million Dollar Value as a professional and have a skillset few people have.

So Lindsey decided to become an expert in wine law. She loved wine and regularly hosted dinner parties with wine tastings. She could take that passion for wine and combine it with her education to become an expert in wine law and represent clients who owned vineyards, restaurants, and other companies who needed her specific, soon-to-be-acquired expertise.

The lesson: the riches are in the niches. Select an industry within an industry to get to know really well, and you can become a really valuable professional who can charge top dollar since you are one of few experts on this particular market.

Okay, but that was just a bonus lesson. The real lesson I want to share is the smart move Lindsey made to give her career a huge head start!

Give Yourself a Start

Here's the genius move Lindsey made as a mere first-year law student: she started a blog. Not just any blog, a blog on wine law. You might think (as I admittedly did at first): Who does Lindsey think she is, starting a blog about wine law when she is only a student? She's not even a lawyer yet! Can non-lawyers write blogs about law?! Turns out, they can.

You see, Lindsey didn't wait for someone else to choose her. She did not wait for someone to give her permission to move in the direction she wanted to go. She just went for it! On July 20, 2010, Lindsey wrote her first blog post. She was very honest about the fact that she was a law student who wanted to learn about wine law, and so she would be sharing her research on the industry on this blog and others could learn along with her.

The blog positioned Lindsey as an expert on wine law (it actually turned her into one—writing about what you're learning reinforces the information and is a legit way to become an expert). It wasn't long before other lawyers and law students started reading her blog. Then folks in the hospitality industry started reading it. She was invited to speak about wine law at conferences. She was invited to write articles for various publications. She was even invited on international trips to tour wine regions in Europe and learn about the legal issues affecting the industry in these countries. All before she even graduated!

During her final year of law school, she was offered a position at a law firm specializing in wine law that would start upon graduation. She had hoped to eventually become a professor of wine law, and she went on to do that too. Years later, Lindsey now has her own practice specializing in wine law and she continues to update the blog.

Madam C. J. Walker once famously said, "I gave myself a start by giving myself a start." That is exactly what Lindsey did. And it's what you should do as well.

Lindsey worked like a millionaire, and in this chapter, I am going to show you how to do the same. What does it mean to work like a millionaire? It means to approach your career with your end goal (your Million Dollar Dream) in mind. Future Millionaires know that their next career move is a stepping stone toward their ultimate goal. That's why you must approach your work strategically and efficiently. Working like a millionaire means networking before you have a job, having a strategy as you apply and interview for jobs, having a plan to negotiate your salary, and exceling at your work so that you earn skills, opportunities, and contacts that can serve you toward your Million Dollar Dream.

Lindsey found a way to capitalize on her expertise and her unique interests (exactly what we discussed in the last chapter), which allowed her to go from simply working a job to doing work that she loves—and gets paid well for. Lindsey didn't wait for her career path to choose her; *she chose it* by giving herself a start with her blog. You can do the same.

If you want to become a TV show producer, can you start producing your own skits on YouTube like Issa Rae did? She created and starred in her series *Awkward Black Girl* on YouTube in 2011. She didn't have enough money to finish the season, so she did a fundraiser on Kickstarter and raised $56,000. Five years later, her first TV series on HBO, *Insecure*, premiered. And it all started with choosing herself and creating her own show on YouTube.

There are many other examples just like this. Your favorite singer, actor, rapper, entrepreneur, and influencer all started at the same place: the bottom. The sooner you begin, the sooner you realize that there are no real barriers to entry except yourself, and you can start the journey toward a successful career right now.

TRY IT: Ask yourself: *How can I position myself as the professional I want to become* ***now****?* Can you start your own show on YouTube? Could you start a podcast on the topic you care about and interview experts in the field? If you want to become an author, could you begin writing stories via a newsletter? What career move could help you become an expert in your chosen niche right now?

For help with this exercise, download the Million Dollar Work worksheet at futuremillionaire.me.

How to Network Before You Even Have a Job

According to LinkedIn, 70 percent of professionals get hired at companies where they already have a connection. And 80 percent of jobs are never posted online. This is called the "hidden job market"—to find out about these jobs, you gotta know someone and get an inside tip or referral. This is why the network-expanding moves that Lindsey and Issa made are crucial. Your network is essential to your ability to get a job.

You may not have much of a network now, but you can create one. Where do you begin? With the people you already know.

When you're just starting out in the working world, you may think you don't have many contacts, and sure, once you get into the workplace, you're going to make more connections than you have right now—but unless you're living all alone in the middle of nowhere, you know people. And those people know people. And somewhere in there, somebody might know about a job that you might like. So when you're starting out on your job search, let people know about it. Let them know what kinds of jobs you're interested in. Check back with them from time to time, especially if your interests change.

You can also ask people in your community to help you set up informational interviews. This is a great way to meet people within your field of interest. Say you want to get into the music business. Maybe you have a friend whose uncle works at a music house, which is a company that helps businesses like advertising agencies find music to use in a commercial. They may not be hiring right when you're looking for a job, but seeking out an informational interview is a good way to learn more about how the business works. Most people are sympathetic to young people trying to break into the working world and they want to be helpful. And if you make a good impression, they're likely to remember you when a position does come up.

Also, get as involved as possible in the industry you're interested in. If it's the arts, go to galleries and venues that support local and regional artists. Volunteer at arts festivals or other industry events. Consider starting a blog or a social media channel devoted to the arts, where you can cover local events and meet other people in the industry.

Connect with people on social media who are involved in the field(s) you're interested in. Consider reaching out to ask them about how they got into the business and hit them up for career advice. Don't be shy about this—most people are happy to discuss their own professional paths. Let's be real, we all like to talk about ourselves!

How to Apply for Jobs

What do you do once your networking turns up a job lead? Or if a job posting online catches your eye? Obviously, you're going to need a resume. But before you go firing off the same document for thirteen different positions, take some time to really consider the job itself and the qualifications the employer is looking for.

The Boys and Girls Clubs of America offers a wealth of career guidance to young people just starting their job search (see appendix), and one of their first tips about résumés is to make sure you're tailoring your résumé to showcase how your skills, experience, and interests align with what *this* particular employer is seeking. Job descriptions should detail not just what your responsibilities were but what you accomplished, worded in ways that speak to the qualifications *of each particular job*. Don't just say that you organized the raffle for your high school's booster club. Make sure they know that you were the top seller, for example, and if you crushed it, then tell them how much you raised, especially if the position you're applying for involves sales.

In addition to work experience, your résumé can highlight volunteer opportunities, clubs and sports you participated in at school, relevant courses (if they align with the job you're applying for, such as being on the robotics team, dominating your computer science classes, or acing automotive repair). Make sure that, within each grouping, you put the entries in chronological order. Have you had any internships? Make sure to include those too, and highlight any responsibilities you had there, as well as achievements you may have earned, that are particularly relevant to the job you're applying for now. Did you win awards in school? Did you get 5s on your APs? Consider adding a section to your resume for "Awards and Honors."

Be sure to educate yourself about how companies evaluate résumés these days, especially if the job you're applying for is with a large company that processes hundreds if not thousands of applications for a wide range of positions. Do your research to find ways to make yours stand out among the masses. But *don't* do it by being cute: no emojis, cartoonish icons, rainbows, unicorns, kittens (I don't care how adorable they are), or any other outlandish stunts on your résumé, people! I'm cringing right now just thinking about it. I know you want to stand out, but don't stand out for the wrong reasons.

Along with your résumé, be sure to create a custom cover letter for every position you apply for. When we are hiring at my company, I always look at the cover letter first. I want to see whether the applicant did their research about our business. Do they know what we do, what we sell, and what our company mission is? Did they read the job description in detail and have a good understanding of what we are seeking in applicants? Did they read my book or listen to my podcasts to get a better understanding of who we are? Are they showing how their experience and education connects to the job opportunity they are applying for? And do they get our company culture and show how their personal values align with our company values?

I know that's a lot of work, especially when you have to do it for every position. Looking for a job can feel like a full-time job. I remember spending a summer applying for jobs in D.C. During the day, I was editing my résumé for twenty-five different jobs a day—all with custom cover letters. At night, I was waiting tables at a nearby restaurant. When I eventually got a job, it was through my network. Someone from my last internship recommended me to a lobbyist who needed an assistant.

Bottom line: Give yourself the best chance by applying to as many jobs as you can with the best representation of you possible via your résumé and cover letter. Then connect with your network as much as possible, as the best opportunities will be found here. *Both and* is the strategy.

How to Interview for Jobs

Did you get yourself an interview?! Yeah, you did! I never doubted you for a second. No need for kooky kitten résumés here; your experience and passion spoke for themselves. Now what?

First, it's okay to be nervous. It's natural to want to make a good impression, and it can be especially nerve-wracking if you tend to be more reserved anyway. Just remember, if you got an interview, the hiring party can envision you in the position. That's a great situation to be in. You deserve this opportunity, so go into that interview confident you belong there. Swagger is the answer, my friend, even if it's just on the inside. Listen to your boldest hip-hop album or whichever Beyoncé or Taylor Swift song gets you hype and strut in there like you are ready to be handed a job.

Even if you're at ease in interview situations, practice interviewing with someone you trust. Practice discussing your experience and what you learned. Practice using those stories to further make the case for why you're the best candidate for the job. Be prepared to answer tough questions ("Tell me about a time you overcame an obstacle" and "What's your biggest weakness?"). Be prepared to discuss why you're drawn to the job. Look for opportunities to showcase your strengths and demonstrate the assets you would bring to the position.

Also, make sure you've done your research about the company before you go into the interview, and have a list of questions to ask your interviewer. Few things show disinterest more than showing up and having zero curiosity about the company or the position! Don't be that person.

You can ask about the company culture. For example: Is everyone remote, hybrid, 100 percent in the office? Are there opportunities for travel or conferences? Are there social functions? Sports leagues? Consider asking what advancement looks like in the company. Are there mentorship programs for new hires? Try to use the interview not just as an opportunity to show them who you are, but also as a chance to learn about this place where you're going to be grinding for the foreseeable future. Don't buy this car without even test driving it, kid!

When you go into the interview itself—even if it's by video call—make sure you present yourself professionally and with confidence. (If you don't feel it, fake it till you make it!) No tank tops, ladies and gents. No cutoffs or athletic shorts. Y'all know this, right?! Some industries are more formal, and a business suit may be the right way to go. For others, such as in creative fields, it may be enough to wear a nice dress or a button-down shirt and a tie. When in doubt, it's always better to be too dressed up than under-dressed. You're showing the interviewer not just who you are right in this moment but also how seriously you're taking this opportunity, and how seriously you should be taken as a candidate. It's like that old shampoo commercial, which is right even if it is goofy: You never get a second chance to make a first impression. So brush your hair, people. And brush your teeth! Show the company in no uncertain terms: you are the one.

Deepak Malhotra, a professor at Harvard Business School who specializes in negotiation, writes in the *Harvard Business Review* about several things to keep in mind when interviewing for a job:[1]

- **BE YOURSELF IN THE INTERVIEW.** This isn't about just being nice or being compliant. (Puhleese don't fall all over yourself trying to be agreeable.) In fact, a potential employer may even want to see that you're comfortable being assertive. But *how* you come across is important. Are you able to state your qualifications with confidence without sounding arrogant? Do you speak with enthusiasm about the current position and company? Are you able to show that you're enjoyable to be around, that you'll make a cordial colleague, but you're not a pushover? Are you forthright, or do you come across as if you're withholding something? Do you sound like you're just trying to say what the other person wants to hear? Are you truly interested in *this* job and *this* company? If they suspect something to the contrary, they may be less open to negotiating a more generous salary, if they even make you an offer. I highly recommend you bring your full, honest self (personality and all!) to the job interview (this does not mean you are acting as comfortable as you do with your besties—use good judgment here). If it doesn't work out, it means it wasn't the right fit for you. You want to work at a place that appreciates the real you.

- **Be engaged.** Use the interview as an opportunity not just to present yourself and your expertise, but to learn more about the company and the potential colleague who is interviewing you. Consider asking about the type of person who has done well in this position in the past. Ask what they themselves like about the company. Be curious.
- **Be an investigator.** In preparation for the salary negotiation, use the interview to investigate how this role adds value at the company and whose life is made easier (or richer) by the person who does this job. Find out what the company's current goals are and how this role can help achieve that overall goal. This will allow you to position yourself as the solution to the company's problem, which can enable you to be paid higher if you're offered the role.

And of course, as important as proper preparation is, the most important thing is to remember that you are worthy of this job. That doesn't always mean that you'll *get* the job, but you are worthy of it. And neither getting it nor not getting it defines your worth. No job defines your worth. Only you can do that.

TRY IT: Applying and interviewing for jobs is a lot of work, but it's doable! I promise you will get through this. Download our Million Dollar Work worksheet for more guidance on applying for and interviewing for jobs at futuremillionaire.me.

How to Negotiate a Salary

Job interviews can be daunting, and if you make it far enough in the process to receive an offer, it can be tempting to take whatever money they offer and skedaddle before they change their minds. I get it—you're young and just starting out. You may not feel like you have much leverage. We've all wished we had the clout to go into an interview shouting, "Show me the money!"

No matter how fearful you are, negotiating is a must. Here's why: According to Fidelity Investments, 58 percent of young professionals do not negotiate their job offers; however, 87 percent of those who do negotiate receive additional compensation.[2] Eighty-seven percent get more money! The odds are ever in your favor.

Furthermore, there is virtually no downside to negotiating. If a potential employer makes you an offer, they're not going to take it away just because you had the nerve to want to make a living wage. (And if they do, major red flag time. They may have just done you a favor. Run.) Plus, it's common to have some wiggle room in the initial pay rate. Most employers expect that there will be some negotiating, but also be prepared for the possibility that the rate is firm and your interviewer may not have the authority to change it. It never hurts to ask, and you won't be penalized for it, so just ask. You just might get it. Even if you don't, you got to stretch your negotiating muscles and practice asking for more. There will be a lot more of that in your future, Future Millionaire, so this is important.

That said, you may feel like the employer has all the power in a salary negotiation, but you're not without leverage, especially if you make a compelling case in the interview for why you're a strong candidate for the job. Here are a few strategies to try:

- **DEMONSTRATE YOUR VALUE.** It's important to go into a salary negotiation prepared to demonstrate why you're not just a good fit for the job, you also deserve the salary you want. Your résumé is a start, but be prepared to discuss how you've excelled in some of the skills the position requires. Can you describe how you've smoothly navigated tricky customer service situations, including how an upset customer later wrote to your manager to praise your efforts? Did you outpace your coworkers in concession stand sales or consistently sell more clothes than anyone else at your retail job? Are your organizational skills so on point that at your last job you Marie Kondo'd the company's supply room and helped saved your boss time and money? If possible, research what the salary is for a comparable position at another company.

- **USE YOUR RESEARCH.** If you've done your job in the interview process, you should understand exactly how the role you are being hired for makes people's lives easier at the company. You should also understand how this role fits into the company's overall goals and mission. Connect your skills and experience to the company's goals and they will be rushing to hire you at the salary you desire. (I know this works because this strategy has worked on me.) For example, if you are being hired as an executive assistant to the CEO and the CEO is working on a major project that will propel the business to greater heights, you might point out how your past experience as an assistant to twelve agents at a busy real estate office makes you more than qualified to get the busy CEO freed up to focus on this big project.
- **SHARE YOUR JOB SEARCH.** Be prepared to be honest about where you are in your job search. You don't have to be specific about where else you're interviewing, but you might be asked if you're entertaining other offers. A prospective employer may be trying to gauge if you'll take the job if it's offered, especially if they improve the starting salary. This is an opportunity to potentially gain leverage in the salary negotiation, so if you are interviewing at other companies, don't withhold that information. If asked, respond confidently and honestly while affirming your interest in the position.
- **BE FLEXIBLE.** Sometimes the interviewer is someone from HR, and they may not have the authority to offer you a higher salary. Or maybe the salary is nonnegotiable because the company has a salary cap. If you can't achieve any movement on the salary itself, consider other areas for negotiation: flexible start date, extra vacation time, the ability to work from home. Maybe you can negotiate getting the

company to pay for a certification program that will help you in the job, or to contribute to the cost of an advanced degree. There's more to an offer than just the salary.

Be flexible too if you reach an item where there seems to be no movement in the negotiation. If this is a job and/or a company you're really excited about, it may be more important to concede the battle and win the war.

For a similar reason, avoid issuing any ultimatums where you can't 100 percent accept the consequences. These rarely put you in a positive light and can actually backfire. In general, don't dig in your heels on a single point and risk souring the relationship, which could pose problems down the line if you accept the job. What may seem like a critical point during the negotiation may actually prove to be of negligible importance to you once you're doing the job. The more important thing is whether it's an opportunity that's a good fit for your journey toward your Million Dollar Dream and a job that you're excited about.

How to Excel on the Job

Once you land a job, start to make yourself invaluable to your employer on day one. Show that you are dependable. Be a little bit early every day—this one thing can give you a reputation of being incredibly reliable. Follow through on what you say you're going to do. Take initiative and look for ways to help or to add value beyond your initial job description (and document them for future salary negotiations). Look for ways you can grow and learn. Seek out new responsibilities and be open to different types of opportunities. You never know how you'll be able to use those skills, that experience, or the contacts you make at some other time. Ask questions, be open to feedback, and take action on the advice you're given.

In the series *Working*, former president Barack Obama offers this simple advice (and it's only three words, so no excuses for not remembering them): Get. Stuff. Done. He describes in the series that no matter how big or small a problem is, he's always looking for somebody who says, "Let me take care of that."

He continues, "If you project an attitude of, 'Whatever it is that's needed, I can handle it and I can do it,' then whoever is running that organization will notice. I promise."

As a business owner, I can attest that this is absolutely true. The reliable people on my team are highly valued at my company and they receive regular raises and/or bonuses to express that appreciation and value. Likewise, the people on my team who often have excuses rather than results are the ones who are let go after a short period of time.

Say yes to opportunities that come up, even if something feels out of your comfort zone. This is a great way to start building leadership skills and show your willingness to take on new responsibilities. Ask to lead the meeting. Say yes to being on the committee. Step up for volunteer opportunities. Take part in extracurriculars. Put yourself in the mix to make important decisions. Volunteer to assist a colleague. Say yes to opportunities simply because you're going to learn things. Ask to sit in on meetings for groups at your company that you may not be part of but that interest you. Observe the skills of those around you. Note when you encounter the kind of leader you admire, and when you're stuck with the kind you *don't* want to be.

When you put yourself into new situations, you're going to grow. You may make mistakes, and you may feel like you don't know what you're doing. Don't shy away from being uncomfortable. Embrace it and know that those challenges are opportunities to grow as a person and become more marketable as a professional. This is how you can make yourself stand out and make the most of any job experience.

How to Negotiate a Raise

If you follow that advice, you're gonna set yourself up to be a highly valued employee. (You would be ah-mazed how easily you can set yourself apart just by being dependable! Get Stuff Done, people.) And then, ta-da, when it's time to negotiate a raise, you've put yourself in a much stronger position.

Before you even go into that negotiation, know your worth. Being young isn't a liability, and you should be paid fairly for the work you do and be able to expect an increase in your salary if you've been doing a good job with excellent results for more than a year without a raise. Try not to be intimidated by the prospect of the raise conversation. I know a lot of you young folks are still learning to use your voices, but put on your big people pants and start advocating for yourselves. You may be costing yourself money if you don't. Besides, assuming you've had positive performance evaluations and you've been reliable, a raise isn't an outrageous request.

When to Ask for a Raise

If your company is performing well, if your performance evaluations have been positive, and it's been more than a year since your salary last saw a boost, it's a reasonable time to initiate the conversation. Bonus points if you can time the discussion to a recent big win or noteworthy accomplishment you've achieved in your job.

If all the above isn't true, then asking for a raise is not your best next step. Requesting a raise backfires when your performance has not been strong, when you've received a raise recently and are asking again, or when the company's overall performance isn't great. (Did somebody say recession?) Instead, improve your performance, wait the full year, and make sure your company is hitting its key metrics too before asking for more.

How to Prepare

If your company doesn't already have a clear policy in place, ask your manager when you can expect a performance review. If there isn't a firm timeline or protocol in place, you can gently jumpstart the process by letting your manager know you'd like to schedule one. Make sure to emphasize not just that you want to discuss your salary, but that you're eager for feedback on your performance and are interested in spotlighting areas for growth. Seeking out additional responsibilities and opportunities for feedback is something you should be doing anyway. (You're doing that already, right?!)

Also, have an idea of the scope of the raise you're hoping for. I mean, there's a raise, and there's unrealistic. Don't go into the negotiation with wild demands—this is probably not the time to ask to use the company jet. But if your job responsibilities have changed significantly or if you've been grinding beyond what's reasonable for the position, you've certainly earned the right to ask for proper compensation. Make sure you can back up your ask. Can you justify and quantify the raise you're going to ask for with specific examples of the extra work you've done or the excessive hours you've worked? Also consider other aspects that may be suitable points for negotiation, especially if you end up not being given a monetary bump. As with your initial salary negotiation, things like vacation days, job flexibility, and education reimbursement can all be potential areas for discussion. (But probably still nah on the company jet, hotshot. That was cute, though.)

Be informed about what a reasonable salary is for your position, your industry, and where you live. Ask trusted colleagues if they are willing to share what they make. You don't have to put them on the spot about their own specific salary, however; frame the question more generally, e.g., "In your experience, what does this kind of position generally pay?" You can use the US Labor Department's website to search average salaries in your city for your position and ask recruiters in your area about general salary levels for positions within your industry.

How to Negotiate Effectively

Repeat after me, people: Know. Your. Worth. First and foremost, be confident about the value you offer, and make sure you have the receipts to back it up. Keep good records of your work history—any accomplishments you've earned, increased sales, value you've added to your team or your department. Proof of your exceptional performance is one of your best assets when it's time to discuss a raise. If you've gotten positive feedback from clients, keep a record of those commendations. Also keep notes, in writing, of any extra days you've worked, any overtime you may have done, or work you've done outside of regular work hours, all of which you haven't been compensated for. When you take on extra responsibilities, note those in your records, as well as promotions. You may not necessarily need to bring these into the meeting with you, but having it clear in your mind helps you be more confident and specific about the value you provide. Don't go into your manager's office swinging. Putting someone on the defensive is rarely an effective negotiating tactic. But being clear, confident, and able to put up the proof can go a long way.

What to Do If You Don't Get a Raise

You're probably gonna be mad, maybe even hurt. That's totally fair. But have your hissy fit at home, not in the middle of your cubicle of sadness. When you get the news, focus on making sure you understand why. If it's because your manager feels like your performance hasn't risen to the level of what the company expects, make sure you know what those metrics are so that you can work on improvements. Ask for specifics, and make note of them. Then keep track of your performance as you reach those milestones so that you can use that in a future negotiation.

If the reason you didn't get the raise is because the company's performance hasn't been as vigorous as your supervisor expected, try to get a sense of when you can revisit the discussion. Ask if there are ways you can help boost that performance. Understand how your position connects to the company's bottom line—ask your manager to discuss it with you specifically—so that you have a sense of how a boost in your performance can boost the company's. Discuss specific goals and ask to have a check-in within a reasonable timeframe (for example, six months later) to reassess. If you're not able to achieve a monetary bump and the reason isn't related to your performance, ask if there are other areas for negotiation, like more vacation days or a hybrid work week.

Make sure to conduct all discussions calmly and resist the urge to take the outcome personally. Often, your manager has to get the greenlight from their own boss for things like a raise, and their hands may be tied. Show professionalism and an openness to grow, while still making it clear that you plan to revisit the discussion in the not-too-distant future. Make sure you have a sense of next steps, whether that's in the form of a future date to revisit the conversation or clear performance goals to work toward.

I know this is a lot to process, and I know it won't be easy (I've been there, y'all, remember!). But I know you've got what it takes to tackle these steps and start making your Million Dollar Work happen. The more prepared you are when it comes to understanding your value, finding your first (or next) job, and negotiating your salary, the better off you'll be to start earning the kind of money that will help you become a Future Millionaire.

All that is left is to get out there and make it happen. Go get 'em, Tiger!

Chapter Summary

- Future Millionaires begin with the end in mind and strategically approach their careers like a stepping stone toward their ultimate goal—their Million Dollar Dream.
- Give yourself a start by positioning yourself as the professional you want to become *now*—start a blog, social media channel, YouTube channel, podcast, event, or other project to position yourself to be noticed by the industry you want to join.
- Eighty percent of jobs are never advertised, therefore who you know matters. Network before you have a job so that you can learn about the opportunities in this hidden job market.
- Be prepared as you begin your job search with a detailed résumé, custom cover letter for every application, and interview strategies like: being yourself while also being professional, being engaged by knowing a lot and asking a lot about the company, and being an investigator to find how the role you're applying for adds value to the company.
- Eighty-seven percent of young people who negotiate their salary receive higher compensation, so plan to negotiate for a higher salary with any and every job offer.
- Position yourself to be a highly valued employee by getting stuff done at work. This will make you eligible for raises and ensure that you earn skills, opportunities, and contacts that can move you toward your Million Dollar Dream.

CHAPTER 9

Build Like a Millionaire

In the last chapter, you learned how to kickstart your career like a millionaire. But if you want to become a millionaire sooner rather than later, moving from employee to owner is an important part of the formula. That's because our greatest chance of becoming a millionaire quickly is as a business owner. While 39 percent of millionaires built their wealth working for someone else, it usually took that group twenty-five years to acquire their average net worth of $3 million. The vast majority of millionaires are self-employed and on average acquired $7 million in net worth in just twelve years.[1] (Yes, my friends, that's more than twice the money in half the time!)

Entrepreneurship is the fast track to wealth—so it's time to build a business. Specifically, a side hustle. Let's get this party started right. And let's get this party started quickly. (You're too young for that reference, but I'm leaving it in. Millennial Author's Privilege.)

What Is a Side Hustle?

A side hustle is a business that you do part time. It's usually a one-person operation—at least, at first. Just you. No other team members. Think: freelancer, contractor, solopreneur, self-employed service provider. Because you don't have any employees aside from yourself, you can keep your business expenses very low and your profit margin extremely high. Most of the cash you make goes directly into your own pocket. (As your side hustle grows, you'll eventually need to hire people to support you.)

But why start a side hustle? While a good paying job that you enjoy doing most of the time is an important step toward your financial future, the truth is that many jobs can set you up for a comfortable life, but not necessarily a wealthy one. The struggle is real. But entrepreneurship is the answer. And you don't have to wait—you can become an owner and start your business now through side hustling.

When you first begin, typically you're already doing something else. You work for an employer, you're in school, you volunteer, or all the above! You've got a full plate. However, you want to get something going on the side to begin building an asset that can produce the long-term wealth you desire as well as produce extra money you can use now, so the effort is worth it.

How to Start a Side Hustle

We've all heard the stories about how some young person started a side hustle in their garage and grew it into a multigazillion-dollar company. Bill Gates, Steve Jobs, Mark Zuckerberg—their stories have become legend. But you don't have to aim for world domination to start a side hustle. And you don't have to be a tech bro either. (Of course, it's okay if you are, *whattup bro!*) You just have to be creative, intentional, and willing to work.

Don't believe starting a business is possible for you? Well, you are wrong. If an eleven-year-old can get a successful company going, you can too! Let me prove it to you.

A MILLION-DOLLAR LEMONADE STAND

Mikaila Ulmer, the founder of lemonade company Me & the Bees, was in sixth grade when she started her company, using her great-grandmother's recipe. Ever since she was four and was stung several times, Mikaila had been afraid of bees. Her mother helped her confront her fear as she got older, challenging her to learn more about bees to better understand their role in nature.

That's when Mikaila learned that the world's honeybee populations were in danger. She realized that she could start a lemonade business and use honey as the sweetener. Even better, she could donate some of her profits to organizations that help protect honeybees.

Mikaila literally started with a lemonade stand in front of her house. Over time, her business caught on, and she started looking for opportunities to expand and grow, including pitching Me & the Bees Lemonade on *Shark Tank*. That smart move earned her a $60,000 investment.

Me & the Bees kept growing from there. Mikaila had a chance to meet then-President Obama at a White House Kids' State Dinner. She's been praised as one of the 10 Innovators of the Year at the South by Southwest festival, and Me & the Bees products are now for sale in Whole Foods and many other stores and restaurants nationwide. All from the humble beginnings of a neighborhood lemonade stand.

As further proof that youth doesn't have to hold you back, Me & the Bees is now a million-dollar company, and Mikaila uses her experience to help other kids start their own businesses. She's also heading to college—where, no doubt, she'll be cooking up even more ventures for the future.

Would you like to own a million-dollar business like Mikaila? I bet you would. And you can! And you don't have to take a huge risk to do it. You just have to get a solid plan in place.

Prerequisite: Look at Your Schedule

How much time do you realistically have to devote to your side hustle? Be mindful of what's aspirational, what's realistic, and what's sustainable. You may think you can devote twenty hours a week to it, but if in reality you can only invest ten, it's better to know that going in so you can set expectations and manage your time accordingly, especially if you're working a full-time job or going to school full-time. You don't want to burn yourself out. But don't count yourself out either! You can choose a side hustle that fits your schedule and is fun and energizing for you. There are many options to choose from, including ones that are not as time-consuming.

Step One: Create Your Million Dollar Offer

I want you thinking like a millionaire CEO even when you're in the early stages of your side hustle, Future Millionaire. That's why I want you to develop a "Million Dollar Offer," not a "Thousand Dollar Offer" or "Hundred Dollar Offer."

Okay, so what's the right offer for you to sell? You probably have a whole list of ideas for things that you could theoretically sell. You could offer dog grooming services, become a private investigator, do family photography, or make T-shirts with funny slogans on them. So many things you could hypothetically do! But how do you figure out which of those ideas should go into the trash pile . . . and which are going to generate tons of cash?

I'm going to teach you a framework to evaluate your ideas and choose the one that is most likely to succeed. Get your pen ready and write this down! It goes like this:

In order to be a Million Dollar Offer, your idea must do the following four things:

1. It must provide a transformation.
2. It must be in-demand.
3. It must be enjoyable.
4. It must be scalable (eventually).

Let me elaborate on each point.

1. It must provide a transformation for your client or customer.

Your offer needs to take your client from Point A to Point B. From disorganized to tidy, from bored to entertained, from unemployed to employed, from frumpy to stylish, from ashy to moisturized, from struggling writer to published author, and so on. It needs to provide a *result*. With Mikaila's business, the transformation she provides is taking her clients from thirsty to quenched with a delicious beverage.

2. It must be in-demand.

In other words, your offer must be something that people actually want. People want: more money, tasty snacks, stylish clothes, fun activities, help walking their dog, and so on. People do not want: uncomfortable chairs, bland cookies, complicated plans, inconveniences, or five-hour Zoom meetings.

Sometimes, you think you know what people want . . . and you are wrong! Even billion-dollar brands get it wrong. You might have an idea that you think is going to be a huge hit, you try it out, and it's not. That's okay! Experimentation is part of the entrepreneurial journey. You may need to test a few concepts in the marketplace before you land on The One that really works.

Mikaila's customers want a delicious beverage made with honey that supports the environment. And we know that because it keeps selling.

3. It must be enjoyable.

Whatever offer you decide to sell, it needs to be enjoyable (like we talked about in chapter 7). It does not need to be the most exciting thing you've ever done in your entire life. It does not need to make you sob with joy. It does not need to be your greatest passion in all of life for ever and ever! It just needs to be *somewhat* enjoyable. It's gotta be something that interests you enough that you will keep showing up to do it.

If you feel totally "meh" about your offer, then it's not a Million Dollar Offer. You will lose interest and give up quickly. You'll struggle to bring this idea to its full potential.

One thing that Mikaila enjoys about her business is saving the honeybees. It's possible she's not that passionate about lemonade, but her passion for honeybees, and the way her lemonade helps to support them, is enough to keep her showing up (even ten years later!).

4. It must be scalable.

Most of the time, when you start a side hustle, you serve your clients or customers one-on-one. But eventually, you hit a ceiling. There are only so many hours in the day, and only so many people you can serve. You max out and there's no room to grow. This is why your offer needs to be scalable. It must be something that can eventually multiply and expand beyond you.

Mikaila used to serve her clients lemonade that she made from scratch in her kitchen and then sold in front of her house, one cup at a time. While this was a great start for her side hustle, it couldn't have made a million dollars that way. Mikaila turned her company into a million-dollar business when she started having her lemonade professionally made and bottled in bulk and began selling it by the shipment to retailers (rather than by the cup to her neighbors).

As we discussed above, the things you enjoy doing in your spare time can also be the things that start bringing in cash for you on the side. Rachel Cargle is now a successful activist, author, and speaker, but when she was in college, she was a babysitter. She was so good at it that she had more babysitting work than she could handle on her own, so she started connecting her friends with babysitting gigs. That went so well that she started a nannying agency that was bringing in a steady income before she even finished school.

You can turn so many hobbies or weekend interests into money-making gigs. If you've got a turntable and an ear for music that gets people moving, you can start a side gig as a DJ. If you've got access to a miter saw and some basic woodcraft supplies, you can sell custom-made picture frames. If you like to bake or sew, you can start a side hustle offering those services.

Even if your best asset is that you have some spare time, there are side hustles you can do with just a little bit of research upfront: you can learn how to mow lawns, for example, or rent a van and remove junk from people's basements or tutor kids in subjects you are naturally good at.

TRY IT: Go back to the list of activities you created in chapter 7. Alongside each item, brainstorm how you might be able to turn that talent or interest into a side hustle. Research side hustles online and make a separate list of side hustles that you wouldn't mind spending some time on if it means earning some extra cash and building a potential empire. If you need a boost coming up with ideas, at the back of the book you will find a list of 100 Ways for Young Adults to Make Money. Review the list and write down the ideas that excite you the most.

Once you have a solid list, consider which ideas on the

list could meet the Million Dollar Offer criteria. Using those criteria, select your top three options.

If you would like more guidance to complete this task, use the Build Like a Millionaire worksheet, which you can find at futuremillionaire.me.

Step Two: Choose Your Ideal Client

When you launch a side hustle, at first you're willing to work with anybody who's got money to pay you. You're not too picky about clients because you just want to bring cash in the door. If a client is your mom, your auntie, your neighbor, a parent from the local PTA, or that one guy you met in the gym locker room who smells vaguely like hard-boiled eggs, whatever! If they have a Venmo app on their phone, you'll work with them!

But fairly quickly, you'll realize that you need to specialize and focus. You need to define, "Who is my ideal client?" Who is this person? What are their needs? Their hopes and fears? Their values? How can you refine your offer so that it delivers *exactly* what this person wants most? The more you focus on serving *one* type of person, the more money you make.

If you're not sure who your ideal client is, no worries! I have a formula for that too. Your ideal client needs to be:

1. someone who will experience a transformation after working with you. From hungry to satisfied, from dry to moisturized, from insecure to confident, and so on. Remember?
2. someone who needs what you offer. Don't try to sell fish to a fisherman! Your ideal client must be someone who needs what you've got.
3. someone you will enjoy working with. You need to like them, respect them, and genuinely care for them. If disorganized people drive you nuts and you don't have compassion for them, maybe don't become a professional organizer.
4. someone who can pay for what you're selling. 'Cause you can't make money if your customers don't pay.

STEP THREE: PRICE YOUR HUSTLE

You have an offer, you have a client, now you need to set your price. Let's discuss how to choose the right price for whatever offer you sell. Spoiler alert: the right price is not the cheapest price.

The first thing I want you to understand about pricing is this: As an entrepreneur, you want to avoid charging by the hour. Instead, you are going to charge based on the value you provide.

Let's say you have a photography side hustle. You specialize in family photography. When someone has a baby, you swoop in, take photos, and commemorate this special time for the family. Your offer includes thirty gorgeous photos of the newborn baby and family delivered in ten days or less. The family loves their photos, and you have captured a priceless personal moment for them. What should you charge for your photography services?

Well, maybe the project took you five hours. You get paid $25 an hour at your day job. Five hours x $25 is $125. So you should charge around $125, right? *Wrong!*

You provided your artistry and expertise to help your client capture this special moment! You delivered the photos quickly so they could send out their baby announcement to all their family and friends in a timely manner. And you're going to charge $125? Over my dead body! Try ten times that amount. I have paid over $1,250 for family photos more than once because having a photographer I am comfortable with when taking photos of my newborn baby is really important to me. I want the photos to come out great the first time because they are only gonna be one week old for one week and I do not want the results messed up. Whatever you offer to sell, whether it's photography, lemonade, dog walking, or tutoring, I want you to charge based on the *value* you provide.

Do not charge based on how many hours it takes to complete the task. Do not charge based on what your competitors are asking for. Do not charge based on what your mom thinks is a good idea. Do not charge based on how much you can afford (your ideal customer has more money than you). Charge solely based on the value you provide.

What are you thinking about charging for your offer? Whatever number popped into your head, scratch it out, because I want you to double it. At *least*. Promise me that you will not undercharge just because you're young.

Madalyn's Story

That well-paid photographer who charges based on value rather than time? That's not a hypothetical story. She's real. And her name is Madalyn Yates.

In fact, Madalyn is not just any photographer, she was *my* photographer for many years. She captured photos of my business events, and important brand moments for my company and my family. I also trusted her with the newborn photos of my youngest child. Every time I hired her, Madalyn did such a good job that I kept hiring her again and again. And let me tell ya, she wasn't charging $125 for her services!

At a young age, Madalyn purchased her first point-and-shoot camera and became the "girl who liked taking photos of everything." After completing an associate's degree in photographic technology (note the marketable skill learned in college!), Madalyn launched her photography business at just twenty years old. Why did she start this business? "I wanted the flexibility to work when I wanted and with whoever I wanted. I wanted to be financially secure to be able to build a life of adventure, purchase a home at a young age, and truly enjoy what I do!" Madalyn's side hustle turned full-time business allowed her to do just that.

Madalyn was so successful as an entrepreneur that she was able to further her wealth-building by buying her own home at the age of twenty-two, just two years after starting her business! In addition to owning her own home, she works when and with whom she wants to, travels often, and has the financial security she wanted to achieve. Dream life: unlocked.

Madalyn's message for fellow young entrepreneurs? "I want business owners to know if I can do it, they can do it. If you have a dream, it's worth chasing after! You can't let anything or anyone get in the way."

Entrepreneurship is the way, and pricing yourself based on value—the way Madalyn has—is essential to your success.

Step Four: Announce Your Hustle

You are ready to hustle! You have an offer, an ideal client, and a valuable price. There's nothing left to do but fling open your doors and tell the world you are here!

If you build it, they will come, right? WRONG! They will not come unless you specifically call them. Repeatedly. Think about it; no one can show up to purchase your product or service unless they know your business exists. That's why you gotta announce your hustle. But you want to be strategic—screaming into the void will not a million dollars make.

Get your first customers by announcing your business to at least one hundred people. Will one hundred people immediately purchase from you? Probably not. But even if just 10 percent of those people say yes, you've got your first ten clients. Cha-ching! Cash in the door. The other ninety people might hire you later, or tell a friend about you, which brings money to you in the future. It's a win no matter what.

How do you announce your business? By sending an email to one hundred people in your current network. Make a list of one hundred people that you already know. Family members, friends, classmates, colleagues, mentors, teachers, former employers, people on your volleyball team, spiritual or faith group, local business owners, etc. Don't leave anyone out!

Send a personal email to each person. You can send five emails per day until you've emailed all one hundred people on your list. Tell them, "I have exciting news! I started a business." Briefly describe your new biz. Ask each person to (1) become a client and/or (2) pass your info along to someone who might need your services. This is exactly how I started my first business—and it's how I got my first five clients in the door.

By talking about your business to one hundred people, you'll get your side hustle off to an excellent start! You will almost certainly get your first ten clients in the door. Go delight those ten clients and provide an excellent experience so they tell all their friends about you. Soon, you'll have people bombarding your inbox with inquiries. "Are you available?" "Can I work with you?" "My friend raved about you." Word of mouth will spread. But in order to create word-of-mouth buzz, first you need to get the party started. Announce your project to one hundred people. Watch what happens next.

TRY IT: Let's get this side hustle going! Here are the steps I want you to take action on right now:

1. Look at your list of top three side hustle ideas. Pick the side

hustle you're most excited about and that fits the Million Dollar Offer criteria.

2. Decide who your ideal client for this Million Dollar Offer is by using the criteria provided above. Write a profile of your ideal client and give them a name to make it real.
3. Decide on the right price for your offer based on the value, not time. When in doubt, double it!
4. Last but not least, write up an announcement and announce your offer to at least one hundred people that you know.

Congratulations! You just created and launched your side hustle!

If you'd like help creating your side hustle, download the Build Like a Millionaire worksheet at futuremillionaire.me.

Once you've got your side hustle started, you'll want to keep going. Here are a few things to think about as you continue to build it up.

1. **Set a goal.** Are you just trying to make enough money to fund a long-awaited vacation or go to a friend's destination wedding? Figure out all the expected costs and determine how much you need to make in order for the trip to happen, then set the goal for your side hustle accordingly. Are you using the side hustle to test the waters for a potentially larger business? Know what the next level you're working toward is. Are you hoping to earn enough to shift from a mobile business to a brick-and-mortar location? Do the research now to know what that will cost, how much you'll need to earn, and what rules and regulations you'll need to accommodate to reach that next tier. Who are the successful players already excelling in the industry? Look for podcasts and articles about their processes and strategies. Set up informational interviews to help you learn about the business directly from folks you admire, and also learn from them about what it takes to scale up your side hustle to the next level. Before you even begin, have a sense of where

you want to go next, and an understanding of how to get yourself and your business there.

2. **ADVERTISE.** Keep the marketing coming! Use every avenue you can think of: social media, emails, word of mouth, and fliers, for starters. Think about the kind of people who are most likely to be your customers. Where do they hang out? Hand out business cards at local shops, farmers markets, community festivals. Tell people in your faith communities and on neighborhood listservs and Nextdoor groups. Advertising doesn't have to be expensive. It just requires you to get scrappy, be creative, and spread the word.
3. **DELIVER.** While there will inevitably be mistakes and missteps, be sure to deliver consistently on your business's promise, whether that's providing the best baked bread, creating error-proof websites, offering reliable landscaping services, or something else. Whatever your side hustle is, do it with pride and diligence. Your reputation is at stake. Make sure you're dependable, consistent, and fair.
4. **INVEST IN YOURSELF.** As you start building your side hustle, look for ways to invest in yourself and your business. Take classes that will add value to the services you offer. For example, if you're a babysitter, take a CPR or first responder class; if you're a fitness coach, look for specialized certifications that can help you offer more value to your clients and allow you to charge more for your services. What are other entrepreneurs in your industry doing to take their business to the next level? How can you keep improving yourself, your services, and your products?

Now What?

So now what? Commit. Choose one thing to focus on and START. You love music? Start advertising your DJ services. Break out the flour and start baking your specialty cookies! Fine-tune your recipes. Get your sweets to the people. Get the word out. Build a fan base. Rinse, repeat.

Think you have a product or service you want to sell? Great! Research how to bring your product or service to market. Talk to other entrepreneurs. Research what else is already out there. Then bring that solution to the marketplace and sell it. *Cha-ching!* The more you focus on one problem, the better you get at solving it and the faster you'll make that coin. The key is to commit to one thing. Try it. See where your interests and your talents lead you.

Chapter Summary

- Millionaires are owners; that's how most of them become millionaires. You can become an owner too by starting a side hustle.
- Don't just sell any offer in your side hustle, sell a Million Dollar Offer. A Million Dollar Offer is one that provides a transformation, is in-demand, is enjoyable for you to deliver, and is scalable (eventually).
- Focus your side hustle on one ideal client who will experience a transformation from working with you, needs your offer, will be enjoyable to work with, and has the ability to pay you.
- Price your Million Dollar Offer based on value, not on time. When in doubt, double your price!
- Announce your offer to one hundred people you know. Ask them to buy it or share it with someone who might like to become a customer. This is how you will get your first few clients.
- Once you've launched your side hustle, continue to set goals, advertise your offer, deliver quality, and invest in yourself. You're on your way to becoming a millionaire, kid!

CHAPTER 10

Manage Money Like a Millionaire

So much of my time as a young adult was spent worrying about money. I would browse bougie department stores and wrack up credit card debt trying to look fancier than I could afford. I overdrew my checking account, missed credit card payments, and torpedoed my credit score. (480, y'all.)

Even when I resolved to rein in my spending, I'd go out to eat with friends and order the cheapest dish—just water for me, skip dessert—only to have everybody else want to split the check evenly. I'd hand over my debit card and say a silent prayer that it wouldn't be declined. Back in those days, I had a front row seat on the struggle bus. I just wanted it all to go away.

Sound familiar?

Clearly, I've figured out a few things since then, and no matter how bad your financial situation is right now, you can too. I also understand if your money fears are deeply ingrained to the point you don't believe in your ability to get out of debt, let alone to prosper. All of those "declines" still haunt me sometimes. The times when my card was rejected felt like a rejection of me, a rejection of my ambitions, a rejection of my efforts to make a better life for myself. It damaged my pride, my confidence, and my belief that things could get better.

But as scary as all this can be, shoving your head in the sand is the worst thing you can do. Millionaires pay attention to their money. They look at it daily. They know where it's going and where it's been. If you're going to be a Future Millionaire, that needs to be you too. Even if there's more air than cash in your wallet right now, you need to know why your money is running off and where it is running off to. Then once you inspect those deets up close, no matter how grim they might be, you need to accept the truth of your situation. And tell yourself, *It's not always going to be like this.* Because it's not.

Here's another fun story about me. After you finish law school, before they send you out into the world, they put you in a room and show you how much debt you have. If you think this sounds terrifying and nausea-inducing, you are absolutely correct. My number? $330k. That included undergrad and law school loans. That's right, I owed $330,000 in student loans. I thought, *No one asked for this cute little activity. Don't tell me that number!* But I knew I had to face it. $330k doesn't just disappear all on its own.

So I got online, connected to a money management app, and loaded it with information about every dollar, every debt, every single thing I was on the hook for. My credit card, my student loans, my checking account. I put it all together and calculated my net worth. The grand total was like negative $300,000-some dollars. The minuses were enormous and the pluses were very little.

If you're in debt right now, I feel your pain. I've lived it. Debt can be deep, dark, and depressing. But your money is not going to stay in whatever purgatory it's in right now. (And if you're not currently $330,000 in debt, great! You're already ahead of the game.)

My first job out of law school, I was making $41,000 a year. If I managed to pay $10,000 a year on my debt, it would still take me like thirty-five years to get everything paid off. So I clearly couldn't just live as frugally as possible, hoping to chip away at the mess until I was debt-free. Getting to a positive net worth came from paying attention to my money, not hiding from it.

So what does paying attention to your money look like?

- **KNOW WHERE IT'S GOING.** Look at your income and your spending. Track it daily. What money is coming in? What's going out? Is it going mostly to Needs? How much is going to Wants? No judgment—what's money for if not to help us have the things we want? But you also need to understand the ebbs and flows of your spending. If too much is flowing out and not enough is flowing in, you need to know that so you can get your money back under control.

- **CREATE MILLION DOLLAR SYSTEMS.** These are systems you set up so that you're managing your money "automagically." The more you schedule things to be automatically handled by software and apps, the more you can focus your time and energy on the things that bring in more money, and the better off you will be.
- **GO TO MONEY CHURCH EVERY WEEK.** What you focus on expands. That's why I highly recommend you carve out time on your calendar each week where you focus on your money. I call this session Money Church. To be clear: Money Church is not about worshiping money. Money Church is a weekly date with your money where you are going to give it attention, take care of any financial tasks, brainstorm money-making ideas, and confront your limiting beliefs around money.

Know Where Your Money Is Going

Back to that $330k I owed. Once I faced that number, I set up a spreadsheet. Most of what I owed was my student loans. But I spent two days digging for every debt I might have, like an old cell phone bill I lost track of and never paid when I closed the account. I was determined to look my finances right in the face. No flinching. I put every single debt in that spreadsheet so that I knew the exact grand total I owed. And then I (slowly) started to pay each debt off one by one.

I also reframed how I thought about that debt. For so long, I had been embarrassed by it. I'd lost count of the number of times I had to talk my way out of overdraft charges and late fees, had to plead my case to some poor customer service rep who probably hung up with me and had to hear it all again on the next call. My low credit score left me with a pit in my stomach. I felt like a failure. But I wasn't, and neither are you.

I've said this before, but it's too important not to say it again. **Debt should not trigger shame.** No matter what our society says, having debt doesn't mean you are stupid, reckless, careless, lazy, or "bad with money."

Most people who are in debt lack money through no fault of their own. Maybe you have debt because . . .

- you value education. You want to learn, grow, and better yourself. Investing in education is a beautiful thing.
- you took a chance on yourself. Maybe you hired a website designer to build a site for your new business. Even if this risk hasn't paid off yet, investing in yourself is brave and smart.
- you care about your family. Perhaps you've made personal sacrifices to help someone you love, like covering a cousin's rent or helping a sibling pay for their school textbooks. Showing up for the people you love is the opposite of careless and stupid.

And keep in mind that if you are from a marginalized group, systems have been in place for centuries to prevent our communities from getting ahead. Slavery, redlining, and the absence of generational wealth are just a few. In addition, when you haven't grown up in a wealthy environment, you're that much less likely to have access to the resources that make wealth building easier. If you don't know how to save or invest, if you don't know how to use credit cards responsibly, if you don't know how to start a business or open a checking account, these things aren't your fault. You haven't been taught. Yet.

TRY IT: Write down three positive things your debt has brought into your life. Did it provide an experience? An opportunity to help a loved one? An object that fills you with joy? Even if the debt represents a costly lesson (maybe you're over there reading this on that mattress you're still paying off), consider what you learned from that mistake. Do you now avoid high interest rates and credit card tomfoolery? That's a valuable lesson learned. By giving your past self grace and finding gratitude in your debt, you can lessen the shame and begin to move toward the great things that are ahead.

Now, this next step might seem strange at first, but you've got to know your starting point. That means determining your net worth. It might feel a little silly to think you have a net worth at your age and in your particular financial situation, but the truth is we all have a number that represents our financial picture. It's called "net worth," but that term implies that if you have a negative net worth, your personal worth is negative too. Hard no. A person's net worth does not reflect their *personal worth*. It's just a number at a particular moment in time. It says nothing about your value as a person. Sometimes that number is in the positive and sometimes it's in the negative. (Remember my negative $330,000?! And I'm for sure a positive $330k and then some as a real person!)

Net worth is the value of your assets minus your liabilities. An asset is anything you own or control that has monetary value. Cash, real estate, stocks, businesses, and savings are all assets. A liability is anything that subtracts from that value. Loans (for example, to purchase a car, a home, or to get an education), credit card balances, and bills that need to be paid are all liabilities.

So if you've got high debt—like I did because of my student loans—and low salary and no other sources of income, that number is going to be a negative. As uncomfortable as it may be, knowing your net worth and tracking it on a monthly basis are important if you want to build wealth. Seeing it once is informative. Seeing how it changes on a monthly basis, however incrementally, will motivate you to make financial decisions that move your net worth in the right direction.

Once you've determined what your net worth is right now, note it somewhere. Write it on today's date on your calendar. Put it on a sticky note on your mirror. Tape it to the lamp next to your bed. That's your starting line, so that weeks, months, years from now, you can see how far you've come. Set up a monthly reminder in your calendar to check in on that number (you can schedule it to happen during Money Church).

Before long, as you see your net worth moving in the right direction, you won't dread checking it—you might be eager to. Maybe you've paid down some debt since you first started tracking it. Maybe you negotiated a raise or earned a freelance bonus. Seeing your net worth move in the right direction will help motivate you to keep making positive changes.

HOW TO OPEN A SAVINGS AND CHECKING ACCOUNT

If you don't already have something set up to store the money coming in (as well as help it grow) and pay off your bills, this section is for you!

You can either go old school or digital—that is, your bank can be in an actual building *in the real world* (how retro!) or you can do the whole thing through an online bank. Sometimes online banks offer higher interest rates for savings accounts and other savings products, so they're worth considering, but OG banks (we oldsters refer to them as "brick-and-mortar") also offer competitive rates and usually have locations all over town, which can be convenient if you need other services later (such as a loan) or prefer to interact with a human. It can also be helpful to bank with an institution that has a wide network of locations in case you need to use an ATM and don't want to incur a fee for using another banks' machine. So do your research and compare the offerings of both to figure out if physical location or online-only is for you.

No matter which you choose, the bank will require certain information from you. Be prepared to show a valid government-issued ID (usually a driver's license, state-issued ID, or a passport) and your social security number (SSN). If you're undocumented and don't have an SSN, banks will accept other identification instead. These include a foreign passport, citizenship card, or school or work ID.

You'll also need to provide your name, address, and date of birth, and sometimes you may also need proof of residency (like a lease or utility bill with your name and address). If you're under eighteen, you will also need a parent or legal guardian who can sign the required legal paperwork.

Usually, you will need to have a small amount of money to open the account. This will be your first deposit.

Whether you open a savings or a checking account (or both) depends on what your plans for the account(s) are. A savings account is a good idea if you're (duh) trying to save up some money, say to build an emergency fund or save for a car or home down payment. Savings accounts have higher interest rates and can be a way for your money to grow passively while you're building it up. Ideally, you'll add to the initial deposit on a regular basis, and it can be immensely satisfying to see the payoff for your hard work as those funds grow. A checking account, on the other hand, is what you'll need for spending—paying bills, making purchases, using a debit card. In either case, look for an account with no monthly fees. You should also make sure the checking account you choose won't clobber you with fees if you overdraw your account. Look for accounts that promise low or no fees for overdrafts. If you open both a savings and a checking account, you can often link the savings to the checking, and the money you have in your savings account can be used to cover possible overdrafts. Which is nice for an accidental account oops, but if you're regularly spending more than you have in checking and having to cover the difference, you'll see your savings stash dwindle, so make sure you know your account balances and don't fall prey to regular overdrafts.

In the end, opening an account can give you a huge sense of agency. It feels good to see what you earn and watch that number grow. You can easily track your spending by monitoring your account activity, and some banks even offer budgeting programs that reflect the comings and goings in your account. So it's an important part of your financial journey.

Set Up Your Million Dollar Systems

You've heard the expression, "Dress for the job you want, not the job you have." Same thing applies to your money. Plan ahead and create systems for the financial life you want, not the one you currently have. This means starting to behave as if you have a million dollars in net worth today. Behaving with the assumption that, one day, you will. People with millions of dollars build systems to manage their money and grow their wealth. Which means you are going to do the same.

Million Dollar Systems: *(noun)* Financial systems set up to track your money and combat scarcity.

If the prospect of setting up a financial system fills you with dread, I want you to reconsider. Yes, it's going to take some work, but think about how good it's going to feel to have a handle on your finances. Think about how good it's going to feel to see the full picture when it comes to your money and know that you have some control over what happens next. You've gotten this far in this book, so I know you can do this.

Also, once more for the people in the back: Shame is not invited here today. Only hope and joy. You're taking control. **The forces trying to hold you back will not hijack your future.** So go into this process feeling proud of what you're undertaking and confident that you're on a path to financial freedom. You've got this. And I promise you, it will be worth it!

TRACK YOUR CREDIT SCORE

A credit score is a three-digit number assigned to you based on your credit history. A credit *report* is the accumulated record of your credit history. Basically, a credit report is like a baseball card for your financial activity: your hits, home runs, RBIs, errors. Except these are stats for things like opening a credit card, applying for a loan, setting up utilities for an apartment or home, starting a job with an employer. It is nearly impossible to exist in our modern world without engaging in transactions that show up on your credit report.

Your credit report paints a picture not just of your financial history but also of your potential reliability to pay your debts. Beyond banks and landlords using your score to assess how dependable you may be, your credit report may be used by insurance companies, who pull it to determine whether to grant you coverage and what rates you'll pay; utility or cell phone companies, to decide whether to provide services; and employers, who may use it to inform their hiring decision. (Note that in this case, they must have your permission first.) Clearly, a less-than-stellar credit history can have repercussions long after you've gotten your financial act together. In fact, negative information stays on your credit report for seven years. If you've declared personal bankruptcy, that stays on your report for ten years. Criminal convictions can stay on your report indefinitely.

Your credit score is an easy shorthand for determining where you stand. According to Experian, one of the three main credit reporting agencies, the average FICO credit score (the one most people refer to) is around 715, which is considered "good" by Experian's metrics. If you have a lot of debt, if you've been late with car loan payments, if you've missed credit card or cell phone payments, or anything along those lines, your score may be lower than that, and you're likely to be perceived as being less financially reliable. (As you can imagine, credit scores don't care about your problems or *why* you missed a few payments. They just reflect the cold, hard truth that you did.)

So when you have a low credit score, this signals (not always fairly or accurately) that you may not be as financially reliable as someone with a higher credit score. Because I can't say it enough, I'll say it again: your credit score (like your net worth) has nothing to do with your value as a human being. But having good credit gives you more spending options, because when you have strong credit, you have more access to capital (i.e., somebody else's money you're able to borrow). And that allows you to do the kinds of things you might not be able to afford on your own, like buy a house, finance a car, or start a business.

What affects your credit score:

- the accounts you have, and how many (e.g., credit cards, mortgages, car loans)
- the age of your accounts (older accounts are usually better, because it signals that you've been paying your bills and are a reliable long-term financial risk)

- the amount of your existing debt
- how timely you are about paying your bills
- how much of your available credit you're using (for example, are you right up at the limit every month?)
- whether there are any outstanding collection actions against you (for example, are you so far behind on payments that the company you owe has turned your debt over to a collection agency?)

How to check your credit score

There are numerous services that will help you monitor and build your credit score, but if you're just starting out, start by viewing your reports through the government website www.AnnualCreditReport.com. This is the official site for free reports as authorized by law. And despite what you may have heard, checking your own credit report will not impact your credit score. Only inquiries about new credit, such as those made by a bank if you're applying for a loan, will affect your credit score.

How to build your credit score

If you've never applied for a credit card or loan, it may be time to start building your credit score. According to Experian, it can take three to six months of credit activity before you establish a credit score. You can build your credit score by:

- applying for a credit card, and (say it with me now) paying the balance on time every month. There are also cards known as secured credit cards that help people who haven't yet had a chance to establish a credit history. I had one of these when I was rebuilding my credit after totally tanking it during college. These cards require a small initial deposit, say $250, which would be used to cover the cost if you miss any payments. As with a regular credit card, the cardholder makes purchases and pays off the balance, and this information is shared with the credit bureaus.
- applying for what's called a "credit-builder loan." Similar to the way a secured credit card holds on to an amount of money as collateral to ensure that you pay your card balance, a credit-builder loan is like

a practice loan. The borrower is "loaned" a small amount of money (often around $1,000) that's put into a savings account, and the borrower makes payments on that amount until they have paid it off, after which they get their money and have had a chance to establish some good credit habits. Note that there may be fees associated with this type of loan.

- opening an account that reports to the credit bureaus (this usually includes most credit cards and loans, but do your research to make sure).

How to improve your credit score

If you have a low credit score, don't despair. There are things you can do to improve it. The Consumer Financial Protection Bureau recommends:

- making your payments on time, every time. Do whatever you can to catch up if you've missed payments, and then make it a priority to stay current. Set up automatic payments if that helps. Set up reminders several days before the bill is due so you don't forget.
- keeping your credit balance as low as possible. Your credit score will be dinged whenever you are using more than 30 percent of the credit you have available. So if you have a credit card with a $1,000 limit, to avoid seeing your credit score go down, don't charge more than $300 on it. If you do, plan to pay it down enough to get the balance under $300 by the time the next payment is due. In an ideal world, you wouldn't carry a credit card balance for more than one month at all. Credit card interest rates are notoriously high, and you're just giving your credit company free money—your hard-earned money—if you're only paying the minimum balance.
- not having too many credit cards. Just because you can get it doesn't mean you should. All credit cards and credit opportunities are not created equal. Don't accept every offer that lands in your mailbox (especially if you're a new college student; to credit card companies, college freshmen are new blood, and they can't wait to prey on their inexperience and thirst for independence). Focus on the cards that offer the lowest interest rates, best terms, and rewards that make sense

for you (like cash back or miles you can save up for your next trip). Websites like NerdWallet and The Points Guy are reputable resources for evaluating the pluses and minuses of various credit cards.

- playing the long game. The longer you're able to demonstrate that you're responsible with credit, the better. Eventually, this habit will be reflected in lower interest rates (which will save you a ton of money whenever you choose to borrow money for a mortgage, car loan, etc.) and a better credit score, as you'll be showing that you have a strong credit history.

Set Up a Budget

In the simplest terms, a budget is a way to know what money you have coming in, track your expenses so you know what money is going out, and make sure you're saving for the future. The particulars of budgeting vary based on your unique situation, and there are many budgeting programs online that can help you set up a budget, like YNAB or Empower. Even just a simple spreadsheet in Excel or Google Sheets will work to get you started. The Federal Trade Commission has a free worksheet on its website that may be a good place to begin (see the appendix for link).

The key is to create a system for keeping track of the money you have coming in, your monthly expenses (those you know you'll have every month as well as the expenses you can't anticipate but want to be prepared for), and your savings goals. Start by gathering all your monthly bills, your bank account statements for at least the past three months, your paycheck stubs, and any other receipts for transactions that impact your finances. Then start dividing your budget into categories. There are the "essentials"—things like rent or mortgage, food, utilities, insurance, transportation (to work or school). Then there are "wants." These are the "nice to have" things that aren't vital for your daily life but provide joy and pleasure (which you deserve; just try not to say, "Treat yourself!" more than your budget can handle and you should be okay). And then there's the "savings" category. Ideally, this is money you set aside each month for the future, whether that's to create an emergency fund for unexpected expenses; to help fund your side hustle; for large purchases, like the down payment on a house or car; or for retirement.

Make updating your budget regularly a habit. I recommended once per week during a session called Money Church (much more on that soon). This is how you'll catch those extra streaming subscriptions you've forgotten about, the *real* number of Uber Eats orders you place each month, the excessive Amazon purchases, etc. It's important to see if there are expenses you can trim, particularly if you are noticing you've spent money on stuff you don't even care about. The key to the right budget for you is spending money on the things that matter to you and spending zero dollars on things that don't. If going to that fancy DJ'd brunch with your friends is really not that important to you, don't allow yourself to be peer pressured into spending money you don't want to.

If you notice your budget has a shortfall or if you are struggling to make ends meet, the key is to earn more money. Your budget will show you the financial difference between how much you are currently earning and how much you want to be earning according to your Million Dollar Dream. Your job as a Future Millionaire is to close that gap one step at a time.

TRY IT: If you don't already have a budget, now's the perfect time to set one up. Follow the steps above and keep track of what you spend for a month. During your weekly Money Church, you can take a good look at how closely your actual expenses align with the budget. Are there areas where you need to trim spending? What tweaks can you make to get your spending and your budget better in line?

For further guidance on setting up your budget, download the Million Dollar Systems worksheet at futuremillionaire.me.

Tackle Debt

As with budgeting, the strategies for dealing with your debt vary widely depending on your particular situation. But in general, you need to create a plan for tackling it. The Federal Trade Commission website (consumer.ftc.gov) lists resources for certain debt situations (for instance, if you're having trouble paying your mortgage or if you're unable to pay your car loan payments). Here are a couple of initial strategies that debt management experts recommend:

- Pay off the debt with the highest interest rate first, then move on the next highest interest rate, and so on.
- Conversely, you can pay off the smallest debt first, to give yourself some momentum, then apply that money toward paying off the next smallest, then apply both of those amounts to paying off the next smallest, and so on.

For debt that feels too large to tackle on your own, there are nonprofit credit counselors who can offer debt counseling for a low or sometimes zero fee.

TO ERASE DEBT, FOCUS ON EXPANDING, NOT SHRINKING. Despite what some financial harpies say, cutting out your daily latte isn't going to make you rich. Your appreciation for avocado toast isn't keeping you broke, for heaven's sake. Forget the online scolds who want to shame you for needing a caffeine fix. This is nonsense and it drives me nuts. (And isn't it interesting that these kinds of critiques are so often lobbed at women and young people? America, your patriarchy is showing.) Enough with the latte rants! Instead of scolding people for spending $1,460 a year on coffee, we could be lifting people up and helping them learn how to make $1,460 more a month. That will have a far bigger impact on people's lives than drinking cheap coffee and suffering a weak caffeine buzz.

Shrinking requires you to cut back on things, trim your budget, pare down expenses. And sure, this can be helpful at times. But you're not going to grow your wealth that way. If you're *expanding*, you're setting aside the same five hours you might spend eliminating things from your expenses, but instead you're using them to come up with a plan to *make* money. You're brainstorming side hustles. You're promoting your business on social media or in your community. You're tapping your network for job opportunities. You're growing your product offerings and increasing your fees accordingly. This is a no-brainer.

One side note about debt: Not all debt is bad. I generally prefer to have little to none of the kind of debt known as "unsecured debt" (which is not backed by collateral and therefore tends to have much higher interest rates). But sometimes you make the calculated risk to take on some debt to help you build your business or fund your education. The kind of debt you want to avoid is the kind that risks putting you in even more financial difficulty down the road—where there's little to no hope of seeing a return on your investment, or where the interest rates are so high that you can't ever pay off the principal because you're only able to chip away at the interest.

Hold Weekly "Money Church"

Now you know how to track your credit, how to set up your budget, and how to tackle your debt. These are the three nonnegotiables of money management. If you can do these three things well, you are on your way to managing the money you earn like a millionaire.

But you are a Future Millionaire—you don't want to just do the bare minimum well when it comes to managing your money. You want to be a pro at money. And how do you make it to the pros? By practicing every week. And that's exactly what you are going to do.

It's time to schedule a very important weekly appointment on your calendar. This appointment is called Money Church. Or, if you don't like that name, call it Hot Money Date or Me 'n My Benjamins or whatever name you want.

Schedule at least sixty to ninety minutes. Every week. Set up a special chime just for your Money Church reminder, phrase it in your calendar like a Bible verse–like pronouncement if you want, just make it a priority. (So spaketh Rachel!) This is your time to light a candle, play your favorite music, and do all the weekly steps we just discussed (look at your bank accounts, check your credit score, assess your debt, and so on). Like a weekly money review.

Money Church is also a great opportunity to take stock of what's been happening in your life lately. Reflect on the last week. What are some Million Dollar Decisions you made that you want to celebrate? What are some Zero Dollar Decisions you (accidentally) made? What are some money-generating ideas you could implement soon?

Here's your exact formula for having a successful Money Church: during the time you've blocked out . . .

1. Look at your money. Log in to your online banking or look at your money-tracking software or spreadsheets. Even if you only have $10 in your checking account right now, there's power in bringing attention to your money and looking toward it instead of looking away. What gets measured gets managed.
2. Go over the numbers and compare them against your budget. How much do you currently have sitting in the bank? How much is flowing into your account soon? Do you have potential money that is likely but not confirmed yet—like a client who wants to hire you but hasn't officially made a deposit? And how much is flowing out? You need to know where your money is coming and going so you know how to make more of it come in and less of it go out! Give yourself props if you stayed within your budget. (Do you guys even say *props* anymore??)
3. Calculate your net worth. This includes examining the financial decisions you've made recently. For instance: saying yes to a tutoring job, raising your prices, selling a car, and so on. What are some Zero Dollar Decisions you've made lately? What are some Million Dollar Decisions you've made too? Which ones have impacted your net worth in a positive way? Which ones have had a negative impact? Forgive yourself for the zero dollar moves—learn, let go, and move on. Celebrate your wins.
4. Write down any patterns you notice and personal "aha" moments you have after looking at the numbers.
5. Spend some time examining your limiting beliefs. What Zero Dollar Story have you been telling yourself lately? Examine those thoughts and reframe them into more helpful, positive thoughts.
6. Use your remaining time to brainstorm new moneymaking ideas and set financial goals. Recommendation: Write down at least twenty-five ideas you have for making more money every month. You don't necessarily need to do all these things. But try to expand your thinking and generate as many possibilities as you can.

7. Come up with exciting rewards to motivate yourself to get moving. Think of how you will reward yourself once you execute one of these moneymaking ideas. For example, your goal might be "I'm going to get three new clients for my dog-walking service this month." And the reward might be "Once I get these three clients, I am going to reward myself with those new running sneakers I've been eyeing."

Do those seven things to have a very successful Money Church session.

Make this a regular, nonnegotiable part of your financial routine. When you hold weekly Money Church, you realize you have more control over your money than maybe you thought. As a bonus, you'll also become more confident about making and managing money. Keep up this practice and watch your prosperity increase tenfold.

Chapter Summary

- Millionaires pay attention to their money. They look at it daily. They know where it's going and where it's been. If you're going to be a Future Millionaire, that needs to be you too.
- Millionaires have Million Dollar Systems set up to manage their money with minimal effort.
- The three key systems you must set up to manage your money well are: 1) tracking and managing your credit score, 2) setting up a budget to manage cashflow, and 3) having a system for tackling debt (yes, even millionaires have debt and use it strategically).
- Millionaires hold weekly Money Church, a weekly date with your money where you are going to give it attention, take care of financial tasks, brainstorm money-making ideas, and confront your limiting beliefs around money.

CHAPTER 11

Invest Like a Millionaire

As much as we want to believe what our hardworking parents taught us, millionaires aren't often made from just hard work. If that was all it took, there would be a lot more millionaires in the world. In fact, there is no shortage of hardworking people all over the world, and yet only 1.5 percent of the world's population are millionaires.[1] So why do some hardworking people become millionaires while other hardworking people don't? It all comes down to one small word with very big impact: risk.

While about a third of millionaires make their money from leadership positions after climbing the corporate ladder (don't forget, this method takes the longest: on average twenty-four years), over 60 percent of millionaires make their money by taking risks. One common risk millionaires take is building a business, as we covered in chapter 9. On average, it takes entrepreneurs twelve years to become millionaires—less than half the time it takes full-time employees. However, it took me seven years to go from starting my business to becoming a millionaire, and many of my clients have done it in less time.

The other common risk Future Millionaires take is investing. In fact, investing generates a lot more money than any form of hard work ever can because we as humans have a finite amount of energy. There is only so much hard work we can effectively do every week without burning ourselves out. But investing allows your money to always be on the clock, exponentially increasing your earning potential with every passing year.

That is why investing is an essential element of your Future Millionaire wealth-building formula.

What I am about to share with you I didn't learn until I was well into my thirties. This is truly the secret to winning the financial game and you're getting it handed to you at your young age. Be proud of yourself for reading this book, then lean in close and pay attention. I am about to show how all the preceding chapters have led you to this moment.

The Get Money Formula

The first step to becoming a Future Millionaire is getting a job, because you have to attain money to live off of and money to eventually invest, and work is the most accessible way to make that happen when you are starting from scratch with zero dollars (where many young people begin, including me). In this first step, you find a job, collect a paycheck, and use most of your paycheck (80 percent) to cover living expenses.

In step one, you want to manage your money from your day job well so you can start to reserve a portion of the paycheck (20 percent) to put toward future investments. Once you have set up your budget and gotten yourself to a financially secure place where you can accumulate a little bit of extra cash from your day job, you'll be ready for the next step.

The second step is to start your side hustle. Your side hustle is an investment in creating an asset—a business—that you own and that is mostly run on your labor. Typically, you are investing a small amount of money (say a few hundred dollars) on startup costs to set up your business. At first, your business provides extra cash for your wants and needs. Eventually, you grow it into a more significant asset: a highly profitable business that you can work on full time, hire other people to work within, and/or sell for a profit.

Step two is your first attempt to separate your labor from your earnings (where the real wealth-building happens). After growing your business for some time, you will start to build a team and see that the business can earn money even when you aren't there. You will begin to have significant excess income that you can use to take the next step toward wealth: become an investor.

In step three, you begin investing some of the profits you made in your business. You can invest in things like the stock market, real estate, other people's businesses, and other kinds of assets. Because investing is not tied to your labor, and due to compound interest (I'll explain this later), there is no ceiling on what you can earn from your investments—whereas there will always be a ceiling on what you can earn from your labor (as we humans can't work twenty-four hours per day, like investments are able to).

That is why as a Future Millionaire, you need to take all three steps to build your wealth. Each step comes with an increasing level of risk, as well as an increasing level of reward. As you might guess, the more risk you take, the greater the possible reward. Does that mean you're gonna jump off a financial-cliff-level of risk right off the bat? Nope! We're going to do this slowly, methodically, and strategically.

	MILLION DOLLAR ACTION	EARNINGS	RISK LEVEL	ROI LEVEL	NEXT STEP
Step 1	Work for a company	Earn a paycheck	Low risk	Low returns	Invest a percentage of your paycheck toward starting a business.
Step 2	Build a company	Earn profits	Moderate risk	Moderate returns	Invest a percentage of your profits in the stock market and perhaps other types of assets.
Step 3	Invest in a company	Earn interest, dividends, and distributions	Moderate to high risk	High returns	Reinvest your returns to earn compound interest.

You've already learned how to obtain and keep a well-paying job and negotiate your salary along the way. You've also learned how to start a side hustle that earns you extra funds to both enjoy your life and make significant investments in your future. Now let's discuss how to invest your excess income to build significant wealth without the additional labor. And I've got great news, because this is where your youth is a huge advantage. Learning how to invest now gives you a giant leg up on making millions. Why? Because of something called compound interest.

Investing in the Stock Market

Investing in the stock market is the most common method people are taught to build wealth. In fact, the number one way Americans become millionaires is through the formula of consistently investing in the stock market, usually in the form of automatic contributions from every paycheck from their employment into a retirement account (like a 401k offered through your job).[2] While this alone can make you a millionaire, it will take well over twenty years to make it happen. If you'd like to become a millionaire sooner, following the Get Money Formula, where you add entrepreneurship into your wealth-building strategy, will get you there a lot sooner.

You may be wondering, *What the heck is the stock market?* The stock market is one of those things where you think you're supposed to know what it is and you feel silly asking, so you stay in the dark, forever confused by this topic. Oh no, Future Millionaire! Not on my watch. This is an important part of your wealth-building strategy, so it's important you understand what the stock market is at a basic level (which is all you need to know!) and how you can use it to build wealth.

To answer your question, the stock market is where investors (that's you!) connect to buy and sell investments. Those investments are mostly stocks, which are shares of ownership in publicly traded companies (rather than privately owned companies, like the one you are going to build as your side hustle).[3] The term "stock market" often refers to one of the major stock market indexes, such as the Dow Jones Industrial Average (one of the oldest and well-known indexes that follows thirty prominent companies listed on the US stock exchanges) or the S&P 500 (or Standard and Poor's 500, which is an index that tracks the performance of five hundred of the largest companies listed on US stock exchanges). When you hear in the news that the stock market is up or down, what's really being reported is that one of these popular stock indexes is up or down. Tracking the performance of every company would be difficult, so these indexes' performance are considered representative of the entire market.

So how do you make money on the stock market? When you buy a stock, you are buying a small piece (or share) of a publicly traded company.

For instance, when you buy Apple stock, you now own a small piece of that company (isn't that cool?). The stock price—i.e., the price of purchasing one share of a publicly traded company—goes up and down every day depending on a variety of market forces. An investor's aim is to make money on this stock price movement. For example, if you would have purchased one share of Apple stock on September 30, 2019, it would have cost you $55.99. Five years later, on September 30, 2024, one share of that same stock was now worth $233. That means by holding on to the stock for five years, you would have seen a $177.01 increase in the value per share that you didn't have to work for. Now imagine you had purchased ten Apple shares for $559.90 or one hundred shares for $5,599 on September 30, 2019. Five years later, your returns would have been $1,770.10 and $17,701, respectively. That is over three times as much as your initial investment (also known as the principal). This is exciting because it allows you to make a stock purchase and watch that purchase value go up exponentially (on average; more on this below), while doing absolutely no additional work.

Bonds are another type of investment you can purchase. When you buy a bond, you are effectively "loaning" money to a company or government for a specified time period, during which you earn interest. When the time period is up, you get your original money back plus that interest. Stocks tend to have higher returns on investment, but they can be riskier because they depend on the value of publicly traded companies, and that value is constantly going up and down. Bonds are more stable, but the amount of money you can make tends to be significantly lower as well.

As a young investor, you have more time to weather instability in the market and recoup losses down the road, so stocks can be a risk that pays off. But diversification—having a good mix of both stocks and bonds—is a stronger investment strategy, because generally when one is down, the other is up, so your finances can weather storms in either.

So how do you actually invest in the stock market? How does one go about buying these stocks and bonds? Anyone can access the stock market through an online brokerage account between the hours of 9:30 a.m. and 4 p.m. EST. Examples of online brokerages where you can set up an account include Interactive Brokers, E*trade, Vanguard, Charles Schwab, Fidelity, and others. To set up an account, you simply go to one of these brokerage websites and follow the instructions to set up your account, and then you can begin buying and selling stocks. If you are under eighteen, you will need a parent or legal guardian to help you set up a custodial account that will revert to your control once you become of legal age.

Setting Up Mutual Funds

Now that you understand what the stock market is, how it works at a base level, and how to set up an account so you can become an investor, I want to share with you my own personal strategy for investing. This is literally how I currently and historically have invested my money for years, and it hasn't failed me yet. Does that mean it's guaranteed to work for you? It certainly does not. In investing, there are no guarantees. Remember, at the beginning of this chapter we talked about how risk builds wealth. Investing always comes with a risk of losing money rather than earning money. That said, there is a way to be strategic with how you invest, in order to minimize risk and increase your chances of seeing significant returns on your investments. That strategy involves mutual funds.

Let's go back to Apple stock. Pretend for a moment that you only own Apple stock. That's the only investment you have. If Apple Inc. has a really bad year, the value of the stock will go down. And that means the value of your entire investment portfolio will also go down. In that case, you would have to wait for Apple Inc. to get it together financially before you would see that stock go up again. Even worse, if Apple were to go out of business (highly unlikely, but nevertheless possible), the value of your stock would be completely wiped out. Likewise, you might find that one of Apple's competitors is doing really well and you are bummed you didn't invest in that stock, where you would have seen big returns. So how do investors avoid this situation, where all their stock value in one company can disappear? Or where they are not invested in other stocks that are on the rise? The answer is mutual funds.

What are mutual funds? According to NerdWallet, "mutual funds are a type of investment that pools together money from many investors, then uses that money to mutually invest in stocks, bonds or other assets. Mutual funds are typically managed by a professional who selects the investments for the fund."[4] That means when you purchase shares of a mutual fund, you are purchasing a basket of stocks put together by a professional fund manager (i.e., someone who knows what they are doing) all at once, which allows you to be immediately diversified. It's like when you go to a restaurant for breakfast and you can't decide if you want pancakes or eggs or oatmeal, so you get the chef-prepared buffet so you can have a little bit of everything. Mutual funds are an investor buffet.

There are two types of mutual funds I want you to understand, because they are key to my personal investment strategy and something I wish I had learned when I was your age. The two types of mutual funds you are gonna want to know are passively managed types called index funds and exchange-traded funds (or ETFs).

Index funds are made up of stocks or bonds listed on a particular index and meant to mirror the risk and returns of that entire index. For example, there is an index fund called Schwab S&P 500 Index Fund (SWPPX, for short). This index fund is meant to mimic what is happening on the S&P 500. That means if the five hundred largest companies tracked by the S&P 500 are, on average, up 2 percent, if you owned shares in this mutual fund, your shares should be up by 2 percent as well.

Likewise, exchange-traded funds are also made up of stocks or bonds listed on a particular index and are meant to mirror the risk and returns of that entire index. The difference between ETFs and index funds is that index funds can only be bought and sold at the end of a trading day, whereas ETFs can trade throughout the day like individual stocks. The price of ETFs fluctuates throughout the day based on real-time supply and demand. ETFs typically have a lower minimum investment than index funds (which means you can get started with a smaller amount of money). The difference between ETFs and index funds is not going to be that important to you as a new investor, but you can definitely educate yourself further on each of these mutual fund types using the resources in the appendix. What is going to be most important as an investor now is that you get in the game.

So what is my personal strategy for investing in the stock market? Buy index funds or ETFs monthly and hold firm. That's it. Simple, boring, effective. Despite what you may have heard, you don't need to know everything about the stock market to become an investor. You don't even need to know everything about mutual funds. Instead, pick a few index funds and/or ETFs that mimic stock indexes and invest a similar amount on a monthly basis (do this through monthly automatic transfers from your checking account to your brokerage account so you don't even have to think about it) and just watch your brokerage account grow. Why monthly? Because it means you are regularly buying stock at the latest price point. If the market goes up, you've purchased at that price. But also, if the market goes down, you've purchased at that price. This can lower your overall average cost per share over time. This is called dollar-cost averaging, and it's a good way to develop a disciplined investing habit, be more efficient in how you invest, prevent your emotions from getting in the way of building wealth, and avoid mistiming the market.

By the way, this is also the investing strategy recommended by most financial experts, *The New York Times*, and many other investing books and resources. Why? Because it's easy, inexpensive (brokerage account fees on index funds and ETFs are usually low), and anyone can do it, even a young person like yourself.

TRY IT: Make your first investment. That's right, I am challenging you to jump in and go for it. The only thing standing in the way of you becoming an investor is overcoming your fear, setting up your brokerage account, and making an initial investment, which could be as little as $50—I bet you've recently spent more than $50 on lunch, a new T-shirt, or an Uber. I want you to be a Future Millionaire, and that means being willing to take a small amount of money you have now, not spend it, and instead put it to work for you by buying a few shares of an index fund or ETF. This is exactly how I started investing—I took a small amount of money and jumped in by buying my very first index fund.

Once you make your first investment, commit to purchasing more shares the following month. Set it up automatically or create a calendar reminder to make this $50 or more investment every month. Then do nothing but sit back and watch the money accumulate. Seeing how your money grows over time is the best investing education you could ever get. It's what will motivate you to earn more so you can keep investing more.

For more guidance on making your first investment, download the Million Dollar Investor cheat sheet at futuremillionaire.me.

Understanding Compound Interest

Now that you have a general understanding of how to invest in the stock market, I want to explain an important concept that is key to understanding how your wealth can grow exponentially once you start investing. That concept is called compound interest.

Compound interest allows your investments to grow faster over time, enabling you to increase your net worth faster too. That is why it's a Future Millionaire's best friend.

Compound interest allows you to earn interest from interest. That is, when you make an investment, you earn interest on your initial investment (i.e., the money you used to purchase the original investment). Then the interest on that initial investment gets added to the principal and you can earn interest on that interest. Earning interest on the principal plus any new interest added makes your investment grow exponentially. This creates the effect of a snowball rolling down the hill and adding more snow as it rolls, getting larger and larger.

Imagine you have purchased shares in a mutual fund. Many mutual funds pay returns to their investors in the form of dividends (dividends are the percentage of a company's earnings that is paid to its shareholders as their share of the profits—decided by the company board and paid out quarterly) and distributions (usually the result of the fund selling some of its assets for a profit—as a shareholder, you get a piece). You can typically take these dividends and distributions in the form of a cash payment made to you or in the form of additional shares in the mutual fund. As a young investor, you will want to reinvest these dividends and distributions in the mutual fund for additional shares (you can do so by simply checking a box on your brokerage account website). When you do that, you unlock the power of compound interest as those dividends and distributions get added to your principal to earn interest as well.

Here's an example from Investopedia to help you better understand how much compound interest can increase your wealth:

Investopedia offered this example as an illustration: A mutual fund opened with an initial investment of $5,000 and subsequent ongoing additions of $200 per month for thirty years. That means you would have invested a total of $77,000 over thirty years. With an average of 12 percent annual return over thirty years, the future value of your investment is $798,500. (Yes, you just turned $77,000 into ten times the amount by just investing and waiting.) What's exciting is $721,500 of the $798,500 value comes from compound interest!

Investopedia notes, "The compound interest is the difference between the cash contributed and the actual future value of the investment. In this case, by contributing $77,000—or a cumulative contribution of just $200 per month over thirty years—compound interest comes to $721,500 of the future balance."[5]

Compound interest is a way to benefit from the sheer amount of time your money is invested. So starting to invest at a young age is an immense advantage when you're building wealth, simply because you're giving that snowball a much longer hill to roll down, and it can pick up a whole lot of snow on the way down. (This is the flip side of how accumulating interest on debt can keep you in a hole that just keeps getting deeper.)

Here's another example of what it looks like to play the compound interest long game. The US Securities and Exchange Commission—the government entity that oversees things like the stock market—has a compound interest calculator on its website that you can play with (see appendix for link). Let's say you're going to invest $500, and you plan to do nothing else to it. You'll make no additional contributions. If the interest rate is 5 percent and you don't touch it for, say, twenty years, that $500 will be $1,326.65. You more than doubled that money by doing nothing more than giving it the gift of time.

Now I know those numbers are not so exciting to a Future Millionaire. So imagine if you kept contributing to that investment. Say you start with that original $500, and now you contribute $50 to the principal every month for the next twenty years. With that same 5 percent interest rate, your initial $500 will now be $21,166.22. Even accounting for the $12,000 you contributed in those $50 increments over twenty years, that's a nice return on your investment!

Far too often, young people see investing as something for older people, or something they'll think about down the road when they're more established in their careers, or when it's not so hard just to pay the bills. Too often, it feels like something that they just can't afford to do right now. But the truth is, if you want to be a Future Millionaire, you can't afford *not* to start now.

Average Stock Market Returns

Okay, so we have done a lot of math in this chapter. However, you are a Future Millionaire, and you're gonna need to be good with numbers given all the money you will be counting in your near future. So let's do a little more math so you have a full understanding of the wealth-building opportunity available to you in the stock market.

When we talk about investing as a society, there is a lot of focus on the risk of losing money. That risk is very real, and so it is important you go into investing with eyes wide open about the possibility of losing money. However, it is also important you fully understand that, on average, the stock market has delivered significant returns to its investors for a century. Yes, that is one hundred years of verifiable history that can give you a great deal of confidence as you embark on your investing journey.

The average stock market return is about 10 percent per year as measured by the S&P index. In some years, the market returns less than that; in other years, it returns more. Ten percent has become the reliable average returns that most investors expect on their investment portfolios.[6] What that means is if you had $1,000 invested in a S&P 500 index fund, you could expect to see your $1,000 investment grow to $1,100 in a year. Does that mean that stock market always delivers 10 percent returns? No, it does not. Sometimes it delivers less and, more often than not, it delivers more. Over the last century, the stock market has grown by a whopping 70 percent!

In addition, investment returns need to be adjusted for inflation, which is the general increase in prices and fall in the purchasing value of money. When those returns are adjusted for inflation of about 2 percent annually, the average returns equal 8 percent (the 10 percent returns minus the 2 percent loss of value to inflation).

Average Stock Market Returns per Year

Average yearly returns on the S&P 500 over the last five to one hundred years*

YEARS AVERAGED (AS OF JULY 31, 2024)	STOCK MARKET AVERAGE RETURN PER YEAR (REINVESTED DIVIDENDS)	AVERAGE RETURN WITH REINVESTED DIVIDENDS AND ADJUSTED FOR INFLATION
100 years	10.628%	6.991%
50 years	11.866%	7.454%
30 years	10.733%	7.803%
20 years	10.473%	7.998%
10 years	12.864%	7.712%
5 years	14.873%	10.308%

* Table adapted from *"Historical Average Stock Market Returns for S&P 500 (5-year to 150-year averages),"* TradeThatSwing.com.

Let's look at a real portfolio of mutual funds for an understanding of how these funds performed against the inflation-adjusted average expectation of 8 percent returns. This is the real-life portfolio of friends of mine from 2023. They own a series of index funds and ETFs in different categories. Here's how their portfolio did in 2023.

As you can see from the table, they got above-average returns in recent years on their portfolio. Does that mean they will always get above-average returns? No. But I hope it illustrates both the opportunity and the risk involved with investing in the stock market. On average, the opportunity tends to be greater than the risk, which is why a majority of Americans (61 percent) have invested in the stock market.[7]

Saving vs. Investing

You might be thinking, *Rachel, I love all of this, but shouldn't I be creating a savings safety net first before I begin investing?* You definitely want short-term savings, where you've got some cash available in case you have an emergency. The money you invested in the stock market is not money you typically want to mess with should an emergency come up. For your short-term savings, open a high-yield savings account. You'll need to shop around to find a bank that offers a significantly above-average interest rate. A high-yield savings account that offers 4 to 5 percent interest on your money is the perfect place to park your short-term savings.

Now, let's talk about how much short-term savings you need. There are lots of financial experts out there who give all kinds of recommendations on how much money you should have saved to protect you if your financial situation changes—say you lose your job and have a tough time finding another one, or you need to take a leave of absence to care for an ill loved one, or you experience some other large financial hit you weren't expecting. I've seen as low as three months of living expenses and as much as one year of living expenses. Here's what I have found: folks who try to save many months of living expenses are rarely able to do so (because needs come up before you ever reach that amount) or it takes so incredibly long that it prevents you from ever getting started with building your investment portfolio.

So here is my (albeit somewhat unconventional) advice: save exactly one month's worth of living expenses in your high-yield savings account. That's right, one month. If you can easily do more, do so, but definitely not more than three months of living expenses. I'd rather see that money earning you compound interest in the stock market than sitting in a savings account, even if it is high-yield. You want all your dollars working overtime for you and earning the maximum amount.

Thirty days is a good amount of time to come up with a plan to replace your monthly income, especially when you are armed with the strategies for starting a side hustle outlined in this book. You know how to make money on demand. In addition to that, have a credit card with at least $1,000 (more, if possible) of available credit on it; use this card only in case of emergencies. Once you have these two things in place, and even before, start investing.

Retirement Accounts

I know, retirement probably seems a million miles away. Trust me, though, time comes at you fast! Resist the temptation to put this off. Your future self will thank you.

Many employers offer a retirement fund called a 401(k)—for nonprofits, it might be a 403(b)—that lets you contribute a portion of your income, pre-tax, into an account that generates interest each pay period. This is actually how most people are investing in the stock market. They allocate a certain percentage of their paycheck to automatically be transferred into their retirement account, where it gets invested. You might feel that you need every bit of your paycheck. I get it. But I'm gonna need you to make this move anyway. In the years to come, you will be so glad you took this opportunity to get a head start that will set you up years from now.

Typically, employers will match what you put into your retirement account up to a certain amount. The average employer matched offered in 2023 was 4.6 percent of your salary.[8] That is free money. Get yours. Over time, this account grows tax-free until you withdraw it in retirement. There is a maximum amount of tax-free money that you can contribute to your 401(k), set by the federal government on an annual basis. In 2023, the maximum amount was $23,500.

If your employer offers a 401(k) or 403(b), always take advantage of this opportunity. This is part of your compensation package, and you won't receive this compensation if you don't open up the account and start putting money into it. Once you have your retirement account set up, follow the advice above and specifically invest those funds in index funds and ETFs. Contribute the max amount to the retirement account that you can afford to each pay period and benefit from the growing compound interest. As your salary increases, increase the amount that you contribute, so that account keeps growing as much as possible.

I want to be clear that, while you want to take full advantage of the opportunity to invest a portion of your salary in your tax-free retirement account, this is by no means all the investing you are going to do. That may be what most people do, but it's not the Future Millionaire way. You also want to have your own separate brokerage account, where you are investing additional funds in index funds and ETFs above and beyond what you put in your employer-provided retirement account.

My First Investment

If all of this seems intimidating, you're not alone. When I first started investing, it all seemed very complicated. I started by reading as much as I could, trying to understand the general language that everybody else seemed to understand already. I took a basic investment class and educated myself so I could go into investing with confidence. I was still feeling intimidated, but the best thing I ever did was begin. One year, I had an extra $4,000. I decided to invest it in an index fund. With fear and trepidation, I opened my first online brokerage account and made my first investment. I purchased VTSAX after reading up on it and learning that it had strong returns over the last ten years. And then I simply watched it. Every week or so, I would log into my account and just see what it was doing. Not much at first. Then eventually I started to see it growing.

It was so cool to see my initial $4,000 investment turn into $6,000 with just a few passing months. That gave me the confidence to start making regular monthly contributions. I started putting in $1,000 per month (I was older when I started, so I had a successful business and could afford to invest this amount every month). Slowly but surely, that account grew and grew and grew. And I got more and more confident increasing my monthly contributions. I have a more robust investment portfolio now, with several types of index funds and ETFs, but my strategy has not changed. Still to this day, I contribute to my various mutual funds monthly and just sit back and watch it grow over time.

This will be your story too. When you follow the Get Money Formula, you are following a proven path not just to a million dollars but to financial well-being. Again, that path is to separate your labor from earning money. You do this by first earning an income in a job, then using a portion of that income to invest in building a side hustle or business, and then take the profits from that business and invest them in the stock market to grow your wealth without your labor. This strategy will not only allow you to enjoy your life, be creative, and have fun, you'll build millions in assets in a sustainable way.

TRY IT: Take some time to dive deeper into investing basics. Write down ten terms you don't know and learn not just what they mean but how they work. Future Millionaires meet challenges head on, so make it a priority to actively work on increasing your financial literacy so that this important part of wealth building is not a mystery.

Part of becoming a millionaire is being willing to take risks—whether that risk is trying out a new career, investing in yourself and your business idea, or wading into investing in the stock market. You will also have to become comfortable with some loss, because no matter which form of risk you take, things won't always go as planned. You will occasionally lose money. You may unexpectedly lose your job, or have stock in a company that folds, or find that your business has a bad year. All these setbacks are part of the process and growth that comes with making money moves, and preparing yourself for them now is an important part of becoming a Future Millionaire. Just like the stock market has ups and downs, you will too. But just like the stock market on average, you will typically see your net worth consistently grow in the right direction.

What's important is that you never let temporary setbacks become permanent by no longer trying. Staying the course on your plan, having faith that everything will work out in the end, is an essential element of your Future Millionaire life.

Chapter Summary

- Investing is an essential element to your Future Millionaire plans, because hard work alone is not guaranteed to make you a millionaire.
- The Get Money Formula includes three steps: 1) Get a job and earn a paycheck, 2) Use your job earnings to invest in starting a business and earn profits, 3) Use the money from your business to invest in the stock market and earn interest, dividends, and distributions, then reinvest your returns to earn compound interest.
- Your investment strategy is simple: buy index funds and/or ETFs monthly and hold.
- Compound interest, which allows you to earn interest on interest, is what allows your money to grow exponentially faster.
- The average stock market returns over the last one hundred years is 10 percent, or 8 percent with inflation. While there is always risk in investing in the stock market, its performance over the years gives investors confidence.
- Saving one month's living expenses in a high-yield savings account and having a 401(k) through your employer are smart financial moves that round out your investing strategy.

CONCLUSION

Your Million Dollar Plan

What I want for you more than anything else is to be a millionaire. According to Henry David Thoreau, "Wealth is the ability to fully experience life," and I want you to experience every last drop.

I want you to experience jumping on a plane and traveling to your dream destination.

I want you to experience your favorite musician in the front row of their sold-out concert.

I want you to experience living in your dream apartment in your dream neighborhood.

I want you to know what it feels like to do work you love and that gives you purpose (working not because you have to, but because you want to).

I want you to know what it feels like to have room in your life for your creative pursuits and quirky hobbies.

And yes, I want you to know what it feels like to have all your bills paid on time while still having plenty left over.

And I want you to know what it feels like to have the money, time, and energy to devote to making other people's lives better (because that's what gives us purpose).

These are the kinds of things money makes possible.

It's never about the money. It's about the options money creates. It's about the freedom money creates. It's about the people money helps. It's about the well-lived life money can make possible.

At the beginning of this book, I told you making money is a learnable skill and one I am going to teach to you. And for two hundred or so pages, I did just that.

Well, hello, Future Millionaire. Now you know.

You know how to dream, think, decide, set boundaries, provide self-care, and friend like a millionaire. And you know how to value, work, build, manage money, and invest like a millionaire.

Knowing is one thing. But knowing alone will not a millionaire make. You must apply all that you have learned in this book. You must do.

So let's get to doing right now.

Your Future Millionaire Plan

Maybe you feel overwhelmed. There are so many things you need to accomplish, and it might feel dizzying! Don't worry, because your Million Dollar Plan is right here. I made a checklist that lays out exactly what you need to do next.

I want you to complete every item on this checklist. It's okay if it takes months or even years to complete. Take your time, but never quit. By doing this, you are putting your plan in motion. You are moving toward the rich, beautiful, and financially secure life you want.

Good news—if you've been following my instructions throughout this book, quite a few of these steps are already done!

Here's your checklist.

- [ ] **IDENTIFY YOUR MILLION DOLLAR DREAM.** This is your highest and best vision for your life. Write down your dream in as much detail as you can. What do you do with your time? How do you earn your money? Where do you live, and who are you hanging out with? Create the full picture of how you want to work, live, and play; who you want to spend your time with; how much money you want to make; and the experiences you want to have.
- [ ] **WRITE DOWN YOUR MILLION DOLLAR WHY.** This is the drive and

motivation behind your Million Dollar Dream. It's essentially the list of reasons why you want to make money and become a millionaire. Keep it somewhere you can refer to it often, like a note in your phone or a sticky note on your desk.

- ☐ **IDENTIFY YOUR TOP THREE ZERO DOLLAR THOUGHTS.** If you're not sure what they are, try paying attention to the things you tell yourself over the next couple of days. Write down new Million Dollar Thoughts to replace each Zero Dollar one. When the negative thoughts come up the next time, acknowledge them, then reconsider them from your new, million-dollar perspective. Practice thought work whenever one of these Zero Dollar Thoughts comes up.
- ☐ **MAKE A MILLION DOLLAR DECISION.** Choose an important decision you need to make and apply the WIN Formula. First, what do you really, truly **W**ant? Think carefully about your **I**ntention—what's the purpose? How will this decision move you closer to your Million Dollar Dream? And what can you do right **N**ow to get started? Write down your WIN so you have these steps right in front of you. Voila! A Million Dollar Decision is made.
- ☐ **CREATE A DECISION LOG.** This is a diary where you list out the key decisions you made. At the end of each month, look back at what you wrote and think through a few key decisions you made that month. The decisions you record can be big ones (like deciding to quit your job) as well as smaller ones (like deciding to return that impulse purchase you made recently). Don't try to track every decision, but list at least three to five decisions you made that month. Once you have some distance from those decisions, ask yourself: Did this turn out to be a Million Dollar Decision or a Zero Dollar Decision? If it was a Zero Dollar Decision, what thinking led to that decision? If it was a Million Dollar Decision, what was the WIN analysis that led to that decision? Doing this will help you to get better and better at making Million Dollar Decisions, which will in turn build your decision-making confidence.
- ☐ **SET MILLION DOLLAR BOUNDARIES.** Assess where you might need to set some Million Dollar Boundaries. Think about what areas of your life are exhausting or disappointing. Write down three to five

things you're sick of doing or areas of your life where you've been settling for crumbs. Where are the time sucks? Who or what is draining your energy? What is drawing down your cash flow? Once you've completed the list, write down what boundary you need to set, who you need to communicate this boundary to, and by what date you will communicate this boundary. For added motivation, write down what you'll be able to do with that extra time, energy, and money you're protecting with your new, healthy boundaries.

- [ ] **DO A TIME STUDY.** Over the course of a week, write down how you are spending your day. What self-care habits are you practicing? What bad habits are sucking up your time or energy? What mental and emotional junk food could you cut from your routine? You may be surprised at what you learn about how you are spending your time, but the beautiful thing is you'll also have the opportunity to do something about it. Once you complete the time study, brainstorm a list of ways you could free up twenty hours per week. Pick at least one idea from that list and do it.
- [ ] **CONDUCT AN ENVIRONMENTAL AUDIT.** Make a note of what isn't working for you and what could be better in your physical, digital, media, and social environments. Then brainstorm a list of low- and no-cost ways you can upgrade them and start making it happen.
- [ ] **DO A FRIENDSHIP AUDIT.** Write a list of the top twenty people you spend the most time with and ask yourself, "Are these people helping me grow and be a better me? Or are they preventing me from becoming the person I want to be?" Look at your answers and consider whether you need to make any changes in terms of who you surround yourself with or how often you spend time with them. Don't be afraid to love someone from afar for the sake of your own life.
- [ ] **PLAN YOUR SUPPORT.** What kind of support do you need in your life? Is it emotional support and camaraderie, professional support and guidance, or some combination of both? Which people can give you that support? Make a list of ideas. Pick one idea from that list and do it today.
- [ ] **CREATE YOUR MILLION DOLLAR SQUAD.** Write a description of your ideal real-life squad. What kinds of people are you looking

for? What do you hope to do together? This can help you articulate exactly what you want from this ideal group. Then choose one thing you will do to bring these kinds of relationships into your life.

- ☐ **IDENTIFY YOUR MILLION DOLLAR VALUE.** List the things that come naturally and easily to you. Write down what you were really good at as a child. List the things people regularly complimented you on. Take another look at your list and add any big accomplishments or milestones you've achieved. Write down any patterns you notice.
- ☐ **TAKE AN ASSESSMENT.** Sign up to take a personality and skills assessment like StrengthsFinder, DISC, Kolbe, or Myers-Briggs. Based on the results of the assessment and the patterns you noticed in the last task, list ten careers you might like to do.
- ☐ **POSITION YOURSELF AS THE PROFESSIONAL YOU WANT TO BECOME.** Brainstorm three ways you can take action now toward the career you want. Then choose one and go for it. Can you start your own show on YouTube? Could you start a podcast on the topic you care about and interview experts in the field? If you want to become an author, could you begin writing stories and sharing them via a newsletter? What career move could help you become an expert in your chosen niche right now?
- ☐ **APPLY FOR ONE HUNDRED JOBS.** Once you have identified the career path you want to follow, research and identify one hundred jobs you can apply for now that would allow you to step into your desired career path. Apply for all one hundred jobs using the advice in this book. When you get interviews, use the advice in this book to ace your interview. When you are offered a position, use the advice in this book to negotiate your salary.
- ☐ **ASK FOR A RAISE.** If your company is performing well, if your performance evaluations have been positive, and it's been more than a year since your salary last saw a boost, it's a reasonable time to initiate the "I'd like a raise" conversation. Bonus points if you can time the discussion to a recent big win or noteworthy accomplishment you've achieved in your job. Follow the instructions in this book to prepare for the discussion, then set a meeting with your boss and request a raise.

- [ ] **Brainstorm Your Side Hustle.** Pull out your Million Dollar Value list. Alongside each item, brainstorm how you might be able to turn that talent or interest into a side hustle. Research side hustles online and make a separate list of side hustles you wouldn't mind spending some time on if it means earning some extra cash and building a potential empire. If you need a boost coming up with ideas, in the back of this book you will find a list called 100 Ways for Young Adults to Make Money. Review the list and write down the ideas that excite you the most.
- [ ] **Create Your Side Hustle.** Look at your list of top three side hustle ideas. Pick the side hustle you're most excited about and that fits the Million Dollar Offer criteria. Decide on your ideal client for this Million Dollar Offer by using the criteria provided in this book. Write a profile of your ideal client and give them a name to make it real. Decide on the right price for your offer based on the value, not time. When in doubt, double it!
- [ ] **Launch Your Side Hustle.** Make a list of one hundred people you already know. Send a personal email to each person. Ask each person to become a client and/or pass your info along to someone who might need your services. Congrats! You just launched your business!
- [ ] **Nurture Your Side Hustle.** Set your company goal and decide how much money you want to make. Continue to do one thing every single week to market your business in order to get the word out and keep bringing in customers. Deliver your product or service to current clients, collect their feedback, and keep improving. Invest part of your profits in your business so that you can continue to grow it.
- [ ] **Track Your Debt and Do a Debt-Forgiveness Ritual.** Create a list of all your current debts, including how much they are, who you owe them to, the monthly payments involved, and relevant account information. Once you have your list, decide which accounts you want to start paying down first. Then write down three positive things your debt has brought into your life. For example: Did it provide an experience? An opportunity to help a loved one? An object

that fills you with joy? Even if the debt represents a costly lesson, consider what you learned from that mistake. Do you now avoid high interest rates and putting too much on your credit card? That's a valuable lesson learned. By giving your past self grace and finding gratitude in your debt, you can lessen the shame and begin to move on to the great things that are ahead.

- ☐ **CALCULATE YOUR NET WORTH.** Add up all your assets (such as savings, stocks, etc.) and deduct any liabilities (such as debt). You can use software to help you. Once you have your current net worth, add it to a spreadsheet or even just a note in your phone with the date you calculated it. Set up a monthly or quarterly reminder in your calendar to recalculate it.
- ☐ **SET UP YOUR BUDGET.** Write down all your monthly, quarterly, and annual expenses and the amount they cost you each month. (You can use software or a simple spreadsheet.) Then plug in your salary and any other income you have. Also add in any monthly savings you'd like to put aside and monthly debt payments you are making. Keep this budget updated and check it monthly against your actual spending.
- ☐ **HOLD WEEKLY MONEY CHURCH.** Schedule a weekly appointment on your calendar for sixty to ninety minutes. During this appointment, assess the status of your money, update your budget, check your credit score, take care of financial tasks, brainstorm money-making ideas, and confront your limiting beliefs around money.
- ☐ **MAKE YOUR FIRST INVESTMENT.** Set up your online brokerage account, choose an ETF or index fund, and purchase shares (remember, you don't need a lot of money to do this). Once you make your first investment, commit to purchasing more shares every month. Set it up to invest automatically or create a calendar reminder to make this $50 or more investment every month.
- ☐ **LEARN ABOUT INVESTING.** Take some time to dive deeper into investing basics. Write down ten terms you don't know and learn not just what they mean but how they work. Select a book, course, or media channel from the appendix to learn from next.

That's your checklist! Tackle one thing at a time. Check things off as you go. Every checkmark gets you closer to the financial abundance that you want.

If you'd like to download this Your Future Millionaire Plan, you can do so at futuremillionaire.me.

There is or will be a moment in your life when you decide, "I'm going to become a millionaire and nothing will stop me." I hope that moment is today. Whenever you do make that decision, you need to make it with 100 percent commitment. Once you do, you're going to approach your ideas, life, and work differently—and your bank account will look different too. There is nothing as powerful as a mind that has been made up.

100 Ways for Young Adults to Make Money

Hey there, Future Millionaire! Whether you're still in high school, navigating college, or just starting out in the working world, it's never too early to kickstart your wealth-building journey. I've put together a list of 100 fun, creative, and profitable activities that can help you start earning now and set you on the path to financial independence. You've got the energy, the motivation, and the drive—now let's turn that into cold, hard cash!

Imagine transforming your passions and skills into a steady stream of income while still having a blast. From teaching voice lessons to selling custom portraits, each idea on this list is a golden opportunity to showcase your talents and fill your wallet. Remember, every millionaire started somewhere, and these activities could be your launchpad to success. So dive in, explore the possibilities, and make your money work as hard as you do. You've got this, and I'm here cheering you on every step of the way!

1. **Become a Social Media Manager**

   Assist a local small business or neighborhood influencers by managing their social media accounts. Help create content and engage with their audience. You'll pick up invaluable skills and build a portfolio of successful campaigns you can use to build your network . . . and your savings!

2. **Virtual Tutoring**

   Offer tutoring services in subjects you enjoy and excel at. Whether it's math, science, writing, or even English as a second language, you can utilize online tutoring platforms to connect with students looking to learn what you already know!

3. **Event Planning**

   Ask your loved ones to hire you to plan the next family BBQ, birthday party, baby shower, or graduation celebration. If you love organizing fun activities and decorating, this is the perfect creative outlet for you that'll help you rake in extra cash.

4. **Become a Content Creator**

   If you're a natural when it comes to nailing TikTok dances and viral trends, lean into it. There are so many people out there right now creating impressive, scroll-stopping content pieces and getting paid to do it. This could be you!

5. **Become a Personal Stylist**

   Have a knack for fashion and style? Embrace it! Offer personal stylist services and help others feel their best for special occasions, vacations, or every day. Curate outfits, design makeup and hair looks, and even offer personalized look books for your clients. Stunning!

6. **Offer Organizing Services**

   Know a friend or family member whose home needs a little TLC? Offer your organization services and assist in cleaning up their closet, pantry, kids' playroom, or office. Charge by the hour and ask your clients to pick up the tab on whatever organizing tools you'll need (shelves, baskets, drawer organizers, etc.).

7. **Flip Furniture**

   Find hidden gems on Facebook Marketplace, Craigslist, Goodwill, or local used stores and give them a new life with paint and new hardware. Then sell the pieces for a profit!

8. **Throw a Garage Sale**

   Clean out your closet, garage, and spaces around the house to find items you no longer need and do a garage sale. (If you're still living at home, get the final okay to sell it!) Make sure to create signs stating the day and place them around your neighborhood, and post about it on yard sale apps/social media to get more people to come out.

9. **Throw an *Epic* Garage Sale**

   Ask friends, family members, and even people around the neighborhood to see if anyone is willing to donate free items to your garage sale to help you really build it out. Set up the lawn by "room" (living room, dining room, etc.) or by "theme" (retro, vintage, like new, etc.) and make it into an experience.

10. **Start a Resale Shop**

   Love thrifting? Launch your *own* thrift shop! Use online platforms like DEPOP or Facebook Marketplace to list and sell your curated used items. From unique clothing and accessories to collectibles and even furniture, business will be booming in no time.

11. **Become a Freelance Writer**

   Flex your composition skills and offer a writing service to anyone who needs help writing blogs, newsletters, websites, bios, and more.

12. **Make and Sell Candles**

   Hit up your local craft store. Pick up wax, wicks, and jars. And create your own candles! Mix and match your favorite scents to create something unique, then sell them to your customers. Launch an online store on Etsy or attend craft shows to sell your new products!

13. **Offer Your Services on UpWork**

   Upwork is one of many platforms that allow you to post about your skills and have people reach out to you directly for work. Or you can browse their list of available jobs and "bid" for the role that fits you the best.

14. **House-sitting**

   House-sit for homeowners while they are away and help ensure the safety of their home while taking care of their plants and pets.

15. **Sell Your Art**

   Go all in on your art. Using sites like Etsy and Society6, you can promote and sell originals or copies of your unique creations to be displayed in your clients' homes and offices! Slap your art on stickers and mugs for even more possibilities.

16. **Build Furniture**

    Get hired to put together new furniture for customers. Using an app like Taskrabbit, share your availability to piece together new shelves, tables, desks, etc., and charge by the hour!

17. **Paint Interiors**

    Offer to help a neighbor paint their house. Charge per room, or by the hour, and do your best work! Make your clients happy with your finished product and they'll recommend you to their friends and family.

18. **Build Custom Computers**

    If you enjoy the creative challenge of building your own computers, then offer to build them for customers too! Enthusiasts are willing to dish out thousands for a totally unique gaming computer. Consider your next big savings goal *met*.

19. **Offer Tech Support**

    Love all things tech? Assist families, friends, teams, and aging adults with technical support and setup services for computers, smartphones, and home networks. Promote your services and offer both on-site and remote support for your new clients!

20. **Become a Gaming Coach**

    Yes—you can get paid to game. Do you know how to beat an extra-tough boss? How to figure out that ultra-complex puzzle? Offer remote coaching services for popular video games and esports titles. Get paid to help others "get good" and beat their favorite games. Everyone wins!

21. **Write Code for a Small Business**

    Love to code? Then you're already ahead of the game. Offer your programming services to local small businesses to help them meet their goals. Get paid and build a strong portfolio you could share as your business grows!

22. **Start a Car Detailing Service**

    Love cars? This is your opportunity to make it into a business. Learn the ins and outs of car detailing from YouTube and get to work. Everyone loves a super clean interior, complete with conditioned leather seats and vacuumed carpets! This involves a bit of an investment, but the payout is extra sweet.

23. **Organize a Car Wash**

Rally some friends together and spend the day washing cars and making money doing it! If you really want to up the value, offer your customers a place to sit and relax, listen to music, and drink some water while they wait for their car. And get a cheap bottle of air freshener to spray in their car to make it smell extra clean for them.

24. **Offer Your Car Wash Service to a Business for a Day**

Find an office building with a parking lot or garage and see if the building manager will allow you to offer car washes to employees while they are at work. Employees who are interested can bring their car to the designated washing station and pay you directly through Venmo or with cash.

25. **Get Paid to Take Photos**

Are you always the go-to person for photos at a party? Do you love taking pictures and playing with different cameras? Turn this hobby into a side hustle by offering your photography skills for family portraits, graduation photos, parties, and more!

26. **Sell Handmade Jewelry**

Love to accessorize with unique handmade jewelry? Make it your side hustle! Piece together stunning works of art your clients can wear. And when they're asked, "Where'd you get that?!" they'll direct people straight to YOU.

27. **Face Painting**

Get creative and offer face painting services at your next neighborhood block party, children's birthday bash, or community event. Your customers will love standing out from the crowd, showing off your celebratory makeup creations!

28. **Help with Chores**

There are a few apps (Taskrabbit, Handy, etc.) that offer services for people who need help around the house, instantly connecting them with someone to help assemble furniture, move large items, do home repairs (like hanging up a TV), and more. If you're a skilled handyman, this is a great avenue to jump into and lend a hand while getting paid for it.

29. **Join a Dog Walking Service**

    Love animals? Then this is a great gig for you! Companies like Rover, Wag, Fetch, etc., offer their customers local pet sitters in their area who can come in and walk their dog while they're at work or take care of their pet when they are out of town, and you can sign up to become one of those sitters.

30. **Pick Up Groceries or Restaurant Orders**

    Help make someone's day a little easier by handling their shopping needs. You can sign up to be a shopper on apps like Shipt and Instacart and use your available time to pick up items on someone's grocery list and drop them off at their doorstep. You can also do easy restaurant pick up deliveries, through apps like Uber Eats and DoorDash.

31. **Become a Plant Designer**

    Yes, this is a thing! If you've got a knack for plants and a passion for design, offer your indoor plant design and maintenance services to spruce up a home and elevate it with your styling skills.

32. **Sell Stationery Designs**

    Love graphic design? Do you hang out on Canva for fun? Then you're sitting on a skill set folks are willing to pay for! Create stationery templates for invitations, holiday cards, and postcards and deliver them digitally via Etsy or Creative Market!

33. **Design Clothes**

    If you're skilled in sewing and designing new fashion pieces, put yourself out there in the market and share your gift with the world. Offer customers the option to order custom pieces or specific color palettes. See if one of your local boutiques would be interested in carrying some of your pieces as well.

34. **Repurpose "Trash"**

    Learn to safely repurpose glass bottles, plasticware, and other household items into flowerpots, home decor, organizers, and more. Sell your items online and at craft shows while also helping decrease the amount of trash in the environment!

35. **Refurbish Electronics**

    If you love to tinker and learn how things work, this is for you. Get used electronics from the thrift store—headphones, keyboards, even computers—and give them a satisfying deep clean. Put them back together while also upgrading some internal components for a just-like-new refurbished item! Sell them on eBay, Etsy, and Facebook Marketplace.

36. **Join a Ride Share Service**

    If you have a car and love driving, you can make some extra money by driving people to their destination through companies like Uber or Lyft. Not only are you getting paid to drive around in your own car, you are able to choose your own hours and the times of day you are available.

37. **Provide Language Tutoring**

    Help others advance in their language skills by offering tutoring sessions for individuals or small groups looking to improve their knowledge in a language you're fluent in.

38. **Play Music**

    Land some extra cash on weekends by busking in popular local destinations (that allow it). Bring your guitar, keyboard, violin, saxophone . . . whatever you play, and perform boldly! Put out an attractive bucket or hat for folks to drop their tips.

39. **Offer Graphic Design Services**

    If you're creative and a master at whipping up graphics for fun, guess what? People will pay for that! You can create visual content such as fliers, posters, or social media graphics for clients.

40. **Consign Clothing and Accessories**

    There are lots of ways to make money while cleaning out your closet. Try consigning—or letting another company sell your clothes for you. Use a website like ThredUp. They will photograph your items and list them. When they sell, you get a portion of the payout!

41. **Create Press-on Nail Art**

    Dive into the colorful world of press-on nail art and let your creativity shine. Custom designs are always in demand, and you can easily sell your unique creations online or to friends looking for a quick and stylish manicure.

42. **Dive into Babysitting**

Pick up a few hours in the evening or on weekends to help friends, family, or acquaintances who need childcare help. Parents are always looking for reliable people who can help take care of their kids and ensure their safety while they are away.

43. **Become a Nanny**

Assist families with childcare on the daily. While the parents are at work or finishing up a project, you can help manage the kids as a full-time or part-time nanny. Play games. Watch movies. Make snacks. And keep kids safe and entertained all day long.

44. **Translate**

If you're skilled in another language, use your multilingual skills to help translate written or spoken content between languages for individuals, businesses, or organizations. Or if someone is in need of an in-person translator for a meeting or event, offer your services and ask to accompany them.

45. **Offer Your Calligraphy Services**

Turn your beautiful handwriting into a lucrative side gig by offering calligraphy services for weddings, invitations, or personalized gifts. Your elegant penmanship can make any occasion extra special.

46. **Offer Voice Lessons**

Share your love for singing by giving voice lessons to aspiring vocalists. Whether they want to nail that audition or simply enjoy music more, your guidance can make a big difference.

47. **Offer Smartphone Screen Repair**

Got a knack for fixing things? Smartphone screen repair is a hot service that can save people from expensive replacements. With a little practice, you can easily turn cracked screens into cash.

48. **Clear Hard Drives**

Help people declutter their digital lives by offering hard drive clearing services. Whether it's organizing files or securely wiping data, you'll provide peace of mind while earning some extra money.

49. Enter Creative Writing Contests

If you have a flair for storytelling, entering creative writing contests can be both fun and profitable. Winning entries often come with cash prizes and the chance to get your work noticed.

50. Write a Book

Make money writing a book—whether it's fiction, nonfiction, an autobiography, comic, poetry compilation, etc.—and make money self-publishing it online. You can use platforms like Amazon Kindle Direct Publishing to get your work out into the world.

51. Get Involved in Affiliate Marketing

Tap into the power of social media and earn commissions by promoting products you love through affiliate marketing. It's a flexible way to make money while sharing your favorite finds with your followers.

52. Make and Sell Pottery

Embrace your inner artist and start creating pottery pieces to sell. From functional mugs to decorative items, handmade ceramics are always in demand and can be sold at local markets or online.

53. Teach Tech

Teach those who are tech-impaired or looking to improve their general computer skills with an online course, one-on-one tutoring, or group lesson. Walk them through the basics of using software programs, enhancing their keyboarding skills, maneuvering through documents, and the key concepts of computer studies.

54. Teach Graphic Design

Share your design skills by teaching graphic design. Whether it's through online tutorials or one-on-one sessions, you'll help others unlock their creativity while earning some cash.

55. Become a Local Tour Guide

Put your hometown knowledge to use by offering guided tours of your city to tourists or visitors interested in learning more about the area.

56. Offer Downsizing Services

Put your organization skills to use by helping older folks who are moving or downsizing to declutter and pare down their things.

While you're offering a valuable service (that you can charge for), you may also feel enriched by the company of someone older, who can share their wisdom and stories with you. And you may be providing them with much-needed company as well. A win-win!

57. Become a Résumé Writer

Help someone secure their next job by creating—or updating—their résumé. Your services can also include editing different versions for specific jobs, as well as helping them to craft compelling cover letters.

58. Become a Résumé Designer

Or if your strong suit is in design, help people design a visually appealing and professional résumé template that will help them stand out when they send in their job applications.

59. Become an Interior Mural Artist

Transform blank walls into stunning works of art as an interior mural artist. Your unique designs can breathe life into any space, making homes and businesses more vibrant and personalized.

60. Become a Brand Designer

Use your eye for aesthetics and branding to help businesses stand out and assert their unique place in the marketplace. As a brand designer, you'll help them determine the way they want to represent themselves to their customers and home in on their company identity. This could include creating logos, color schemes, and marketing materials that tell compelling stories, attract customers, and set them apart from their competitors.

61. Give Music Lessons

For the musically inclined, you can pass along your skills and techniques by giving music lessons. Teach others how to play an instrument you know (piano, guitar, trumpet, drums, etc.) or help them improve their musical talents, offering either private lessons or group classes.

62. Find a Job as a Photography Assistant

Gain hands-on experience and make some extra money by working as a photography assistant. You'll learn the ins and outs of the trade while helping photographers capture perfect shots at events, photoshoots, and more.

63. Do Alterations

Alterations at fancy shops can cost a lot! If you've got a knack for this, offer to do clothing alteration and tailoring services for individuals who need modifications on clothes, zippers, dresses, curtains, etc.

64. Become a Keepsake Resin Artist

Preserve memories in beautiful resin art by creating keepsakes in the form of jewelry, coasters, and decor. Your custom pieces can capture special moments and make for cherished gifts.

65. Record Guided Meditations

Share your soothing voice and calming presence by recording guided meditations for apps like Insight Timer. Help people relax, focus, and find inner peace while also earning tips.

66. Upsell Things

Buy and refurbish items you found at a garage sale, Goodwill, or local buy/sell/trade groups. Use your keen eye and a little elbow grease to transform one person's castoff item by giving it a fresh coat of paint, a new slipcover, or a resewn silhouette, creating something unique and beautiful. You'll be giving an old item new life, saving it from the landfill, and making money at the same time.

67. Take Surveys

Make your opinions count by taking online surveys. Companies value your feedback and will pay for your insights on products, services, and trends, making it a simple way to earn extra cash in your spare time.

68. Sell Custom Portraits

Help people capture special moments and personalities by creating custom portraits. Although we're in a time when it's never been easier to take photos of ourselves and loved ones, most of these images live on a hard drive and few make it to keepsake status. Brainstorm ways to turn portraits into cherished keepsakes. Images can be printed onto blankets, turned into framed wall art, or even made into wallpaper. As the chief creative officer, you'll help people envision how beloved portraits can become cherished keepsakes.

69. **Offer Feedback on New Websites**

Get paid to surf the web by offering feedback on new websites. Your insights can help businesses improve user experience and functionality, making the internet a better place for everyone.

70. **Offer Transcription Services**

Help convert audio recordings into written text by providing transcription services for podcasts, interviews, or meetings.

71. **Become a Personal Shopper**

If you've got an eye for fashion and shopping, consider offering your personal shopping services to help clients select and purchase clothing or gifts based on their preferences.

72. **Meal Prep for Others**

Detail-oriented meets foodie. Prepare and deliver homemade meals or meal kits to busy individuals and families, or anyone who needs that extra hand and is looking for convenient dining options.

73. **Put Your Green Thumb to Use**

Provide gardening or landscaping services like planting or yard cleanup for homes or commercial properties.

74. **Work as a Personal Assistant**

Many busy entrepreneurs and professionals look to hire a personal assistant who can assist beyond the clerical calendar details. Get a job working as a personal assistant and help bring ease to their life by running errands, picking their kids up from school, booking personal appointments, etc.

75. **Grow and Sell Succulents**

Turn your green thumb into a profitable hobby by growing and selling succulents. These trendy, low-maintenance plants are perfect for dorm rooms, offices, and homes, making them a hit with buyers.

76. **Pick Up Jobs on Facebook**

There are so many random opportunities that can fit your skill set . . . and Facebook is a hub for it! Search the endless options in the Facebook groups, such as: Jobs for Digital Nomads, Creative Jobs for Writers, etc.

77. **Edit TikTok videos**

Leverage your editing skills to help content creators shine on TikTok. With your knack for timing and creativity, you can turn raw footage into viral-worthy videos that grab attention.

78. **Explore Sport Coaching**

Offer your services to teach beginners how to improve in a sport you're skilled at. For example, offer tennis or golf lessons at the local club, or offer to coach a kids' basketball team.

79. **Teach Yoga**

Share your passion for wellness by teaching yoga classes. Whether it's in a studio, park, or online, you'll help others find balance and strength while making money doing what you love.

80. **Design Ads to Promote Others**

Are you creative and good at selling things? Use that skill to get paid helping others craft the perfect ads for their business—be it a video they can post online or a printed piece they can mail out to potential customers. And if writing is your thing, you can also craft the perfect headlines to catch people's attention.

81. **Offer Remote IT or Electronic Support**

Put on your expert hat and provide remote IT support services, such as troubleshooting computer issues, performing software installations, or fixing network connectivity problems. Or join a local business that offers this as an additional support (like the Geek Squad).

82. **Become a Researcher**

Authors, journalists, professors, and more are always on the lookout for great researchers to help them dive deeper into a topic or pull up specific stats. If sleuthing is your thing (aka, you're an ace in the game Clue) and Google is your best friend, use your skills to help bring organization and direction into their project.

83. **Offer Your Services as a Fact-checker**

Put your research skills to good use by working as a fact-checker. Whether it's for articles, books, or marketing materials, your attention to detail ensures accuracy and reliability.

84. Sell Unique Crystals

Dive into the mystical world of crystals and sell unique pieces to collectors and enthusiasts. Each crystal has its own story and properties, making them popular for both decoration and spiritual practices.

85. Become a Virtual Assistant

Provide remote administrative support for someone and help them manage their calendar, respond to emails, and handle customer inquiries for their business.

86. Do Voice Acting

Showcase your vocal talents and range and land a paid gig providing voice acting services for commercials, animations, video games, and audiobooks.

87. Sell Niche Imports

Discover unique products from around the world and sell them as niche imports. Whether it's exotic snacks, handmade crafts, or trendy fashion items, there's always a market for rare and interesting finds.

88. Become an Event DJ or MC

Flex your love for music by being a DJ at parties, weddings, or events. You can curate playlists, play music, make announcements, and elevate the energy to make sure guests are having a great time.

89. Offer Refreshments Near Local Sporting Events

Set up a refreshment stand near local sporting events* and quench fans' thirst. Offering cold drinks and snacks can be a lucrative way to capitalize on the crowd's energy and excitement. (*Of course, always check local regulations about vending licenses first.)

90. Sell Character Art

Bring fictional characters to life with your art and sell character illustrations with your added creative touch. From anime to superheroes, your creations can find a home with fans who appreciate your talent.

91. Model for a Local Brand

Use your style and presence to model for a local brand. Whether it's fashion, accessories, or lifestyle products, you'll help bring their vision to life while gaining exposure and income.

92. **Become an Elderly Companion**

Everyone needs a friend! Provide companionship and assistance to elderly individuals by offering social interaction and basic caregiving support. Take time to get to know them and ask them to share stories from their life. You'll be surprised what you'll learn and how fulfilling this can be!

93. **Offer Data Entry Services**

Find a local business or a business online that is looking for a detail-oriented person to help them with inputting, updating, and maintaining data records.

94. **Offer Podcast Editing**

If you're the techy type, consider helping edit and produce podcasts for content creators or businesses.

95. **Become a Personal Chef**

Are you a future chef wanting to practice your skills with an audience? Put the word out there that people can hire you for their next party or event or even a special date night at home, and wow folks with your incredible kitchen skills.

96. **Offer Fitness Training**

Help clients achieve their fitness goals by hiring you to design their workout plans. You can also offer personal training sessions or lead group fitness classes.

97. **Provide Remote Customer Service Support**

If you love talking on the phone, this is the place for you. Work with a business to provide customer support via phone, email, or website chat to assist in their customer service needs.

98. **Become a Home Decor Consultant**

Put your interior design skills into motion by offering home decor consultation services to give advice and recommendations for improving home aesthetics. Bonus: have them hire you to execute the vision and bring it to life!

99. **Take Notes**

Offer your services as a note-taker for meetings or courses. Your organized and detailed notes can help busy professionals and students stay on top of their tasks and studies.

100. Help People Organize Their Finances

Show others how to get their financial life in order by organizing their finances and creating budgets. Your expertise can guide them toward better spending habits and financial stability.

Appendix

Chapter 5

Job search & career advice: https://www.bgca.org/programs/career-development

Questions to ask in an informational interview: https://www.bgca.org/news-stories/2022/December/7-questions-to-ask-in-an-informational-interview

Résumé tips: https://www.bgca.org/news- stories/2023/September/resume-tips

Negotiating: https://hbr.org/2014/04/15-rules-for-negotiating-a-job-offer

Chapter 7

CliftonStrengths assessment: https://www.gallup.com/cliftonstrengths

DISC Test: tonyrobbins.com/disc

Kolbe test: https://www.kolbe.com

Myers-Briggs Type Indicator test: https://www.mbtionline.com

Chapter 8

Boys & Girls Clubs of America job resources:

- Workforce Readiness programs: https://www.bgca.org/programs/career-development/

- Interview Tips for Teens: How to Be First Job Ready: https://www.bgca.org/news-stories/2024/August/interview-tips-for-teens-how-to-be-first-job-ready

Chapter 10

Federal Trade Commission budgeting worksheet: https://consumer.gov/sites/default/files/pdf-1020-make-budget-worksheet_form.pdf

Chapter 11

US Securities and Exchange Commission compound interest calculator: https://www.investor.gov/financial-tools-calculators/calculators/compound-interest-calculator

Resources for educating yourself on mutual funds (specifically ETFs and index funds):

- Nerdwallet.com
- Investopedia.com
- *The Bogleheads' Guide to Investing* by Mel Lindauer, Taylor Larimore, and Michael LeBoeuf (Wiley, 2nd edition; 2021)
- Our Rich Journey YouTube Channel: youtube.com/ourrichjourney
- Invested Development, a course on investing by Amanda Holden: https://amandaholden.podia.com/invested-development
- Stock Market Investing for F.I.R.E.: https://www.ourrichjourney.com/investingforfire
- https://www.npr.org/series/1190516050/planet-money-summer-school-investing

Notes

Chapter 2

1. Tom Corely. "Seven Thinking Habits of Self-Made Millionaires." Richhabits.net blog post, March 20, 2024. https://richhabits.net/seven-thinking-habits-of-self-made-millionaires.

Chapter 5

1. Rubin A, Mangal R, Stead TS, Walker J, Ganti L. "The extent of sleep deprivation and daytime sleepiness in young adults." *Health Psychology Research*. 2023;11. https://doi:10.52965/001c.74555.

Chapter 7

1. Arthur C. Brooks. "Jung's Five Pillars of a Good Life." *The Atlantic,* April 11, 2024. https://www.theatlantic.com/ideas/archive/2024/04/carl-jung-pillars-life-happiness/678009/?utm_source=newsletter&utm_medium=email&utm_campaign=the-atlantic-am&utm_term=The+Atlantic+AM.
2. Ibid.
3. Ibid.

Chapter 8

1. Deepak Malhotra. "15 Rules for Negotiating a Job Offer." *Harvard Business Review,* April 2014. https://hbr.org/2014/04/15-rules-for-negotiating-a-job-offer.

2. "Fidelity Study Shows Young Professionals on the Move: Six-in-Ten Have Changed Jobs During the Pandemic or Expect to Be at a Different Company Within Two Years." Fidelity Newsroom, December 24, 2022. https://newsroom.fidelity.com/pressreleases/fidelity-study-shows-young-professionals-on-the-move--six-in-ten-have-changed-jobs-during-the-pandem/s/30fcad9c-a822-4b51-8f1a-1a61915a6b2e, accessed August 13, 2024.

Chapter 9

1. Tom Corley, Rich Habits Research Study

Chapter 11

1. Marium Ali and Hanna Duggal. "Where are the world's millionaires and how is wealth divided globally?" Aljazeera News, https://www.aljazeera.com/news/2024/7/27/where-are-the-worlds-millionaires-and-how-is-wealth-divided-globally#:~:text=The%20world%20has%20at%20least,92%20percent%20of%20global%20wealth.
2. Danny Noonan. "The Number One Way Americans are Becoming Millionaires." Morningstar, https://www.morningstar.com/financial-advisors/number-one-way-americans-are-becoming-millionaires.
3. Definition adapted from Chris Davis and Sam Taube's "What Is the Stock Market?" Nerd Wallet, https://www.nerdwallet.com/article/investing/what-is-the-stock-market.
4. Alana Benson. "Mutual Funds: What They Are and How They Work." Nerd Wallet, https://www.nerdwallet.com/article/investing/mutual-funds.
5. Justin Walton. "What Is the Link Between Mutual Funds and Compound Interest?" Investopedia, https://www.investopedia.com/ask/answers/100715/how-do-mutual-funds-compound-interest.asp.
6. James Royal and Arielle O'Shea. "What Is the Average Stock Market Return?" Nerd Wallet, https://www.nerdwallet.com/article/investing/average-stock-market-return.
7. "What Percentage of Americans Own Stock?" Gallup News, https://news.gallup.com/poll/266807/percentage-americans-owns-stock.aspx.
8. Tim Parker. "What Is a Good 401(k) Match? How It Works and What's the Average." Investopedia, updated July 29, 2024. https://www.investopedia.com/articles/personal-finance/120315/what-good-401k-match.asp.

About the Author

Rachel Rodgers is the CEO and founder of Hello Seven, a company that teaches women, BIPOC, and LGBTQIA people how to build a seven-figure business and create generational wealth. And she's interested in helping the next generations start off on the right financial footing at a young age.

Rachel is the author of *We Should All Be Millionaires: A Woman's Guide to Earning More, Building Wealth, and Gaining Economic Power*, a *Wall Street Journal*, *USA Today*, and Amazon bestseller, which has also been named one of Audible's top audiobooks of 2021, with more than 200,000 copies sold. Her other books include *We Should All Be Millionaires: The Workbook* and *Future Millionaire*, as well as *Plan Your Year Like a Millionaire*, *Million Dollar Habits*, and *Six-Figure Side Hustle* (Audible Originals).

You've also likely seen Rachel sharing her tips on business, money, and mindset on *Good Morning America*, *The Drew Barrymore Show*, and *Live with Kelly and Mark*, in addition to *The New York Times*, *Forbes*, *Entrepreneur*, *Inc*, Cheddar, PopSugar, and *Women's Health*.

Her mission is to help you end the cycle of overworking, under-earning, and financial stress—once and for all.

An attorney turned entrepreneur, Black woman, working mother, and self-made millionaire, Rodgers brings powerful insights combined with personal stories from her climb to the top. She's known for her blunt advice and for calling out the elephant in the room—whether it's racism, misogyny, or centuries of unfair legal practices that stripped financial power away from women and people of color. Rodgers teaches her clients how to make millions in spite of the very real obstacles in their path.